GIFTED GAMES™

COGAT® TEST PREP • LEVEL 8

Revised Edition With Updated Introduction & 300 Questions

Gateway Gifted Resources™
www.GatewayGifted.com

Thank you for selecting this book. We are a family-owned publishing company - a consortium of educators, test designers, book designers, parents, and kid-testers.

We would be thrilled if you left us a quick review on the website where you purchased this book!

The Gateway Gifted Resources™ Team
www.GatewayGifted.com

TABLE OF CONTENTS

INTRODUCTION

WORKBOOK

PRACTICE QUESTION SET

ANSWER KEYS & DIRECTIONS FOR PRACTICE QUESTION SET

ADDITIONAL BOOKS AND FREE EBOOK INFORMATION

CHILD CERTIFICATE

ABOUT THE COGAT® LEVEL 8: The COGAT® (Cognitive Abilities Test®) Level 8 is given to children in second grade. As the name suggests, it assesses your child's cognitive skills. The test is divided into 3 "batteries." Each of the batteries has 3 question types. The Verbal Battery's question types are Picture Analogies, Picture Classification, and Sentence Completion. The Non-Verbal Battery's question types are Figure Analogies, Figure Classification, and Paper Folding. The Quantitative Battery's question types are Number Analogies, Number Puzzles, and Number Series. Each question type has 18 questions, except for Paper Folding and Number Puzzles, which have 14 questions each. The test has 154 questions total. The test, about two hours in length, is administered in different testing sessions. Children are not expected to complete 154 questions in one session. **See p.6-9 for more on these question types.**

ABOUT COGAT® TESTING PROCEDURES: These vary by school. Tests may be given individually or in a group. These tests may be used as the single factor for admission to gifted programs, or they may be used in combination with IQ tests or as part of a student "portfolio." They are used by some schools together with tests like Iowa Assessments™ to measure academic achievement. Check with your testing site to determine its specific testing procedures.

ABOUT THIS BOOK: This book introduces cognitive skill-building exercises to early elementary-age children through child-friendly subjects. The format is designed to help prepare children taking standardized multiple-choice gifted and talented assessment tests like the COGAT®. This book has five parts.

1. Introduction (p.4-9): About the COGAT® and about this book (p.4); Test Taking Tips (p.5), The Kids' Detective Agency (p.5), and Question Examples & Explanations (p.6-9).

2. Workbook (p.10-48): Pages 10-48 are designed similarly to content tested in the COGAT®'s nine test question types. The Workbook exercises are meant to be done together with no time limit. **Before doing the Workbook with your child, read the Question Examples & Explanations (p.6-9).**

3. Practice Question Set (p.50-90): The Practice Question Set helps children develop critical thinking and test-taking skills. A "score" (a percentile rank) cannot be obtained from this. (See below for more on gifted test scoring.) It provides an introduction to standardized test-taking in a relaxed manner (parents may provide guidance if needed). It is an opportunity for children to practice focusing on a group of questions for a longer time period (something to which some children are not accustomed). It is also a way for parents to identify points of strength/ weakness in COGAT® question types. It is divided into three sections to mirror the three COGAT® batteries: Verbal, Quantitative, and Non-Verbal.

4. Directions and Answer Keys (p.91-95): These pages contain answer keys for both the Workbook and the Practice Question Set. They also include the directions to read to your child for the Practice Question Set. To mimic actual tests, the directions are separate from the child's pages in the Practice Question Set. Cut out these pages.

5. Afterword (p.96): Information on additional books, free eBook of practice questions, and your child's certificate

QUESTION NOTE: Because each child has different cognitive abilities, the questions in this book are at varied skill levels. The exercises may or may not require a great deal of parental guidance to complete, depending on your child's abilities and familiarity with this multiple choice question format. Most sections of the Workbook begin with a relatively easy question. We suggest always completing at least the first question together, ensuring your child is not confused about what the question asks or with the directions.

"BUBBLES" NOTE: Your child will most likely have to fill in "bubbles" (the circles) to indicate answer choices. (Check with your testing site regarding its "bubble" use.) Show your child how to fill in the bubble to indicate his/her answer choice using a pencil. If your child needs to change his/her answer, (s)he should erase the original mark and fill in the new choice.

SCORING NOTE: Check with your school/program for its specific scoring and admissions requirements. Here is a general summary of the scoring process. First, your child's raw score is established. This is the number of questions correctly answered. Points are not deducted for questions answered incorrectly. Next, this score is compared to other test-takers of his/her same age group (and, for the COGAT®, the same grade level) using various indices to then calculate your child's stanine (a score from one to nine) and percentile rank. If your child achieved the percentile rank of 98%, then (s)he scored as well as or better than 98% of test-takers. In general, gifted programs accept scores of *at least* 98% or *higher*. Please note that a percentile rank "score" cannot be obtained from our practice material. This material has not been given to a large enough sample of test-takers to develop any kind of base score necessary for percentile rank calculations.

TEST TAKING TIPS

• Have your child practice listening carefully. Paying attention is important, because test questions are not repeated.
• In the Workbook section, go through the exercises together by talking about them: what the exercise is asking the child to do and what makes the answer choices correct/incorrect. This will not only familiarize your child with working through exercises, it will also help him/her develop a process of elimination (getting rid of any answer choices that are incorrect).
• Make sure your child looks at **each** answer choice.
• Test-takers receive points for the number of correct answers. If your child says that (s)he does not know the answer, (s)he should first eliminate any answers that are obviously not correct. Guess instead of leaving a question unanswered.
• Remind your child to choose only ONE answer.
• Remember common sense tips like getting enough sleep. It has been scientifically proven that kids perform below their grade level when they are tired. Feed them a breakfast for sustained energy and concentration (complex carbohydrates and protein; avoid foods/drinks high in sugar). Have them use the restroom prior to the test.

THE "KIDS DETECTIVE AGENCY"

To increase engagement and to add an incentive to complete exercises, a detective theme accompanies this book. The book's characters belong to a detective agency. They want your child to help them solve "puzzles" so that your child can join, too! If your child completes all the book's questions, (s)he will "join" the detective agency. Feel free to modify the number of pages/exercises your child must complete in order to receive his/her certificate (p. 96).

The Kids' Detective Agency

We're the Kids' Detective Agency. We need another member, and we think YOU have what it takes to join us.

Detectives in the Kids' Detective Agency figure out puzzles and find answers to questions.

To prove you're ready to join us, you'll put your skills to the test in this book. Together with your mom, dad, or other adult, you need to solve puzzles. The adult helping you will explain what to do - listen carefully!

A good detective:
• Pays attention and listens closely
• Looks carefully at all choices before answering a question
• Keeps trying even if some questions are hard

Your parent (or other adult) will tell you which pages to do. After finishing them all, you will become a member of the Kids' Detective Agency! (Remember, it's more important to answer the questions the right way than to try to finish them really fast.) After you're done, you'll get your very own Kids' Detective Agency certificate.

When you're ready to start the puzzles, write your name here:

_____

QUESTION EXAMPLES & EXPLANATIONS This section introduces the 9 COGAT® question types through <u>basic</u> examples and explanations. In each question type (#1-#9), show your child the example (one basic example question consisting of images), then read the directions aloud. After the directions there are additional explanations for parents.

VERBAL BATTERY

1. Picture Analogies Directions: The pictures in the top boxes go together in some way. Look at the bottom boxes. One is empty. Next to the boxes is a row of pictures. Which one goes with the picture in the bottom box like the pictures in the top boxes do?

Explanation Your child must determine how the top set is related. Then, (s)he must determine what answer choice goes in the box with a question mark so that the bottom set has the same relationship as the top. It's helpful to come up with a "rule" describing how the top set goes together. Take this rule, apply it to the bottom picture and determine which answer choice makes the bottom set follow the same "rule." If more than one choice works, then you need a more specific rule.

Here is a tire and a car. A tire is part of a car. A tire is found on a car. A rule would be, "the thing in the first box is found on the thing in the second box. The first thing is part of the second thing." On the bottom is a leaf. Try the answer choices with the rule. An acorn is not correct because a leaf is not part of an acorn, nor is a leaf found on a grasshopper, nor on the sun. A tree is correct because a leaf is found on a tree. A leaf is part of a tree.

These simple examples are an introduction to common analogy logic. Read the "Question" then "Answer Choices" to your child. Which choice goes best? Note that all logic is *reversible*. For example, "Part: Whole" could also be "Whole: Part."

Analogy Logic	Questions	Answer Choices (Answer is Underlined)			
• "X": Opposite of "X"	On *is to* Off -as- Hot *is to* ?	Warm	Sun	<u>Cold</u>	Oven
• Part: Whole	Toe *is to* Foot -as- Petal *is to* ?	Stem	Bee	Leg	<u>Flower</u>
• Animal: Its Home	Bird *is to* Nest -as- Bat *is to* ?	<u>Cave</u>	Fly	Night	Wing
• Animal: Its Food	Seed *is to* Bird -as- Acorn *is to* ?	Nut	Peanut	<u>Squirrel</u>	Worm
• Animal: Its Covering	Bird *is to* Feathers -as- Fish *is to* ?	Swim	Sharks	Tails	<u>Scales</u>
• Baby: Adult	Duckling *is to* Duck -as- Chick *is to* ?	Goose	<u>Rooster</u>	Egg	Hatch
• Object: Item Used to Consume It	Soup *is to* Spoon -as- Drink *is to* ?	Liquid	Juice	Fork	<u>Straw</u>
• Vehicle: Worker	Police Car *is to* Police Officer -as- Spaceship *is to* ?	Rocket	Planet	<u>Astronaut</u>	Doctor
• Object: Location	Sun *is to* Sky -as- Swing *is to* ?	<u>Playground</u>	Monkey Bars	Fun	Up
• Similar: Similar	Turkey *is to* Parrot -as- Ant *is to* ?	Worm	<u>Beetle</u>	Duck	Crawl
• Food: Its Source	Honey *is to* Bee -as- Egg *is to* ?	Farm	Beehive	Round	<u>Chicken</u>
• Object: Creator	Painting *is to* Artist -as- Furniture *is to* ?	<u>Carpenter</u>	Tool	Chair	Potter
• Object: Container	Ice Cube *is to* Ice Tray -as- Flower *is to* ?	Petal	<u>Vase</u>	Smell	Florist
• Tool: Worker	Paintbrush *is to* Artist -as- Microscope *is to* ?	Telescope	<u>Scientist</u>	Lab	Fireman
• Object: Its Shape	Ball *is to* Sphere -as- Dice *is to* ?	Line	Oval	<u>Cube</u>	Cone
• Object: Action You Do When Using It	Microphone *is to* Talk -as- Binoculars *is to* ?	Hear	Speak	Spell	<u>See</u>
• Whole: Part (Materials to Make a Home)	Anthill *is to* Dirt -as- Cabin *is to* ?	<u>Wood</u>	House	Person	Sand
• Object: Location (Vehicles)	Jet *is to* Sky -as- Canoe *is to* ?	Boat	Land	<u>Water</u>	Sail
• Object: Where It's Used	Chalk *is to* Chalkboard -as- Paintbrush *is to* ?	Artist	<u>Easel</u>	Museum	Eraser

2. Picture Classification Directions: The top row shows pictures that are alike in some way. Look at the bottom row. Which bottom picture goes best with those on top?

Explanation Come up with a "rule" describing how they're alike. Then, see which answer choice follows the rule. If more than one choice does, then try a more specific rule.

Here are shoes, gloves, and dice. At first, it may be hard to see anything they have in common. Let's look closer. They each show a pair. This is how they are alike. The first and second pictures do not show a pair (a fan and bubble mix). The last choice, ice cream scoops, shows three scoops, not two. The third choice shows the correct answer – a pair of socks. Everyday life presents an opportunity to improve classification skills, as themes for Picture Classification (and Picture Analogies and Sentence Completion) include (but are not limited to) this list of common classification logic (gray font). Under the logic is an example question. Read the first list of 3 words to your child. Then, next to it, read the 4 choices to your child. Which one of the choices goes best with the first list?

• function and uses of common objects (i.e., writing and drawing / measuring / cutting / drinking / eating)
Fork / Chopsticks / Knife   Choices: Stove / Kitchen / Meat / <u>Spoon</u>   (Used For Eating)
• location of common objects
Refrigerator / Cabinet / Table   Choices: Bed / Restaurant / <u>Oven</u> / Shower   (Found In Kitchens)
• appearance of common objects (i.e., color; objects in pairs; objects with stripes vs. spots; object's shape)
Ketchup / Blood / Firetruck   Choices: <u>Cherry</u> / Mustard / Cucumber / Police car   (Red)
• characteristics of common objects (i.e., hot, cold)
Ice / Igloo / Popsicle   Choices: Cookie / <u>Snowman</u> / Palm Tree / Coffee   (Cold)
• animal/human homes
Aquarium / Barn / Nest   Choices: Feather / <u>Beehive</u> / Farmer / Fish   (Animal Homes)
• animal types
Leopard / Cheetah / Kitten   Choices: Elephant / Giraffe / <u>Tiger</u> / Bat   (Cats)
• natural habitats
Swamp / River / Pond   Choices: Desert / Mountain / House / <u>Ocean</u>   (Water)
• food types
Cake / Bread / Donut   Choices: Sherbet / <u>Cookie</u> / Syrup / Sugar   (Baked Foods)
• food growing location (i.e., on a tree, under the ground as a root, or on a vine)
Potato / Carrot / Onion   Choices: <u>Radish</u> / Melon / Pepper / Broccoli   (Root Vegetables)
• professions, community helpers
Doctor / Fireman / Vet   Choices: Witch / Wizard / <u>Teacher</u> / Baby   (Community Helpers)
• clothing (i.e., in what weather it's worn; on what body part it's worn)
Crown / Cowboy Hat / Cap   Choices: Necklace / <u>Helmet</u> / Gloves / Ring   (Worn On Head)
• transportation (i.e., where things travel, land/water/air; do they have wheels?)
Cruise Ship / Yacht / Kayak   Choices: <u>Canoe</u> / Fisherman / Dock / Jeep   (Travel On Water)

Additional topics include seasons and weather, sports objects, basic solar system knowledge (i.e., about the sun, moon, Earth), appearance of animal babies vs. adults, and musical instruments.

<u>3. Sentence Completion</u> Directions: Listen to the question, then choose your answer. (Each question has different directions.) Max sees something floating in the water. Which one does Max see?

Explanation The first choice, a rock, doesn't float, neither does a hammer or a coin. A beach ball does float in water; it is the answer. Your child must listen carefully. Test administrators will read the question only one time. To practice listening, remind your child to listen to **all** directions, from start to finish. Some kids stop paying attention when they think they know the answer. Build knowledge related to the list of themes in Picture Classification (which also helps with Picture Analogies).

NONVERBAL BATTERY

<u>4. Figure Analogies</u> Directions: The pictures inside the top boxes go together in some way. Look at the bottom boxes. One is empty. Next to the boxes is a row of pictures. Which one goes with the picture in the bottom box like the pictures in the top boxes? (The word "picture" here actually refers to a "figure" that can consist of shapes, lines, etc.)

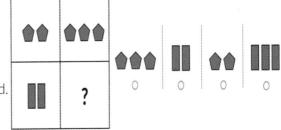

Explanation Come up with a "rule" describing how the top set is related. This shows how the left box "changes" into the right box. On the left are 2 pentagons. On the right are 3 pentagons. The rule/change is that one more of the same kind of shape was added. On the bottom are 2 rectangles. The first choice is incorrect because it shows 3 pentagons - not the same shapes as the bottom box. The second choice is incorrect - it only shows 2 rectangles. The third choice is incorrect - it has 2 pentagons. The last choice is correct - there are 3 rectangles (1 more of the same shapes that were in the left box).

Here's a list of frequent "rules" / "changes" in Figure Analogies. Easier questions involve one "change," while more challenging questions involve more than one change (see example #9 below).

1. Color

2. Size

3. Rotation 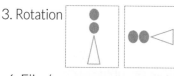 *Notice how much it rotates and the direction (clockwise vs. counter-clockwise): 90° counter-clockwise.*

4. Color Reversal

5. Amount

6. Flip / Mirror Image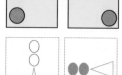

7. Whole: Part

8. Number of Shape Sides

9. Two Changes: Rotation & Color 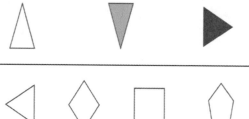 *Compare to #3 (where it only rotates) - here the 2 circles change color also.*

5. Figure Classification Directions: Look at the top row of pictures. These pictures are alike in some way. Look at the bottom row. Which picture on the bottom goes best with the pictures on top?

Explanation The "pictures" in the directions refer to figures. Try to come up with a "rule" describing how the figures in the top row are alike. Then, see which choice follows the rule. If more than one choice would, then a more specific rule is needed. Here is 1 white triangle, 1 lightly shaded triangle, and 1 dark triangle. These are alike because they are all triangles. The first choice is correct because it's a triangle. None of the other choice (B, C, D) are triangles. If you get "stumped" by any of these, then try asking these kinds of questions:

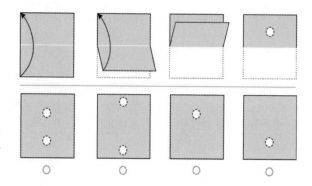

• If there are 3 main figures (above), how many sides do they have?

• If there are 3 main figures, are they made of straight lines or are they rounded?

• If there are 3 main figures, are the shapes flat or 3-D?

• What direction are the figures facing?

• If the figures are different colors or if the figures have dots/lines inside, what do these look like?

• If the figures are divided, how are they divided?

• If each of the 3 figures is actually made of a group of shapes, how many shapes are in the group?

• If each of the 3 figures is actually made of a group of shapes, where are the shapes within the group?

• If each of the 3 figures is actually made of a group of shapes, is there a particular order of the group of shapes?

6. Paper Folding Directions: The top row of pictures shows a sheet of paper, how it was folded, and how something was cut out of it. Which picture on the bottom row shows how the paper would look after its unfolded?

Explanation The first choice shows how it would look - 2 holes in the correct position. In the second choice, the holes are too close to the edge. In the third and fourth choice, there's only 1 hole. (Even though you only see 1 hole in the top row, when the paper is unfolded, there will be 2.) Here, holes have been cut out. However, other questions have different shapes cut out. Also, some questions will show paper that has been folded more than once.

Pay attention to: the number of objects cut out, where these objects are on the paper, and the direction they are facing. Try demonstrating with real paper. For example, you could do the first few Paper Folding questions (starting on p.32) using real paper and a hole puncher or scissors. Seeing real-life examples will assist children with correctly envisioning the paper folding steps during the test.

QUANTITATIVE BATTERY

7. Number Series Directions: Which rod would go in the place of the missing rod to finish the pattern?

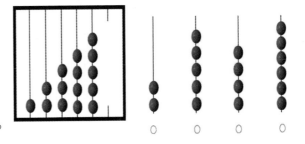

Explanation The last abacus rod is missing. Before it, the rods have made a pattern that your child must figure out. Then, "complete" the pattern with the correct answer choice. Young kids will frequently miscount the beads, so first, ensure they are correctly counting the beads. Looking across the abacus, from left to right, we see that with each rod the number of beads increases by 1. The rods go: 1–2–3–4–5–? This means that the missing rod needs 6 beads (Choice D).
Here is a list of common logic patterns found in Number Series questions. This book has examples of all of these.

Logic	Number of Beads	Logic	Number of Beads
1 bead is added	(0, 1, 2, 3, 4)	1 bead is taken away	(5, 4, 3, 2, 1)
2 beads are added	(0, 2, 4, 6, 8)	2 beads are taken away	(6, 4, 2, 0)
A-A-B-A-A-B	(3, 3, 2, 3, 3, 2)	A-B-C	(3, 2, 1, 3, 2, 1)
A-A-B-B-C-C	(3, 3, 2, 2, 1, 1)	A-B-C-zero-C-B-A	(6-3-2-0-2-3-6)

A / X / A+1 / X / A+2	(1, 0, 2, 0, 3, 0, 4) (here "X" is 0, it gets repeated every other time)
A / X / A-1 / X / A-2	(8, 1, 7, 1, 6, 1, 5) (here "X" is 1, it gets repeated every other time)
A / B / A+1 / B+1 / A+2 / B+2	(1, 5, 2, 6, 3, 7) (the first, third, fifth number & the second, fourth, sixth number increase by 1)
A / B / A-1 / B-1 / A-2 / B-2	(7, 3, 6, 2, 5, 1) (the first, third, fifth number & the second, fourth, sixth number decrease by 1)

8. Number Puzzles Directions: Look at the box that has the question mark. Which number would go here so that both of the sides of this equal sign (point to the equal sign) would have the same amount?

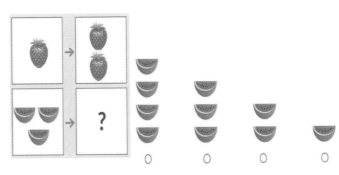

Two plus five equals seven. So, Choice C (5) is the correct answer.

Practice basic math equations together to build Number Puzzles skills.

9. Number Analogies Directions: The pictures on top go together in some way. Look at the bottom boxes. One is empty. Next to the boxes is a row of pictures. Which choice goes with the bottom box like the pictures on top do?

Explanation Number Analogies are similar to Picture/Figure Analogies, but now the top set and the bottom set must have the same mathematical relationship. In the left box there is 1 object (a strawberry). In the right box there are 2 objects. From left to right, we see that 1 object has been added. So, the rule here is "1 is added" or "+1." In the bottom left box there are 3 objects. If our rule is "1 is added," when you have 3 and you add 1, you get 4. (3 + 1 = 4.) Choice A is the correct answer. Many of these questions involve addition and subtraction. However, some questions will involve dividing a group of objects (p.47 #10), as well as halving (p.45 #3), doubling (p.45 #4), and tripling (p.46 #6).

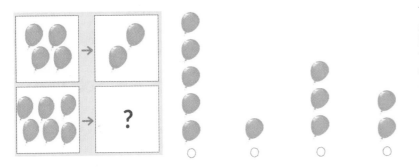

Tip: If you think a rule is to add or subtract on top, and find that none of the choices work with the bottom left box, then try to double or triple (if the top boxes increase from left to right) or halve or divide by 3 (if the top boxes decrease from left to right). On the left, from the top boxes, you may have come up with the rule "take away 2" (4 - 2 = 2). However, 6 - 2 = 4, but there is no answer choice with 4. In a case like this, try to halve (or divide by 3). Half of 4 equals 2. Half of 6 equals 3 (Choice C).

LET'S HELP FREDDIE FIGURE OUT WHAT GOES IN THE EMPTY BOX!

Directions: Look at these boxes that are on top. The pictures that are inside belong together in some way. Then, look at these boxes that are on the bottom. One of these boxes on the bottom is empty.

Which answer choice goes together with this picture that is in the bottom box like these pictures that are in the top boxes?

Parent note: Analogies compare sets of items, and the way they are related can easily be missed at first. Work through these together with your child so (s)he sees how the top set is related. Together, try to come up with a "rule" to describe how the top set is related. (The small arrows show that the pictures belong together in some way.) Then, look at the picture on the bottom. Take this "rule," use it together with the picture on the bottom, and figure out which of the answer choices would follow that same rule. For answer choices that do not follow this rule, eliminate them. If your child finds that more than one choice follows this rule, then try to come up with a rule that is more specific.

Example (read this to your child): In the first box there is a whistle. In the second box there is a mouth. (Talk about the two pictures and try to come up with a "rule.") In order to use a whistle, the body part you mainly use is your mouth. What is in the bottom box? It is a magnifying glass. Now, let's look at the answer choices. Which one goes with the picture of the magnifying glass in the same way that the pictures in the top row go together?

An eye. In order to use a magnifying glass, the body part you mainly use is your eye.

1.

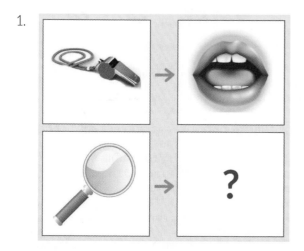

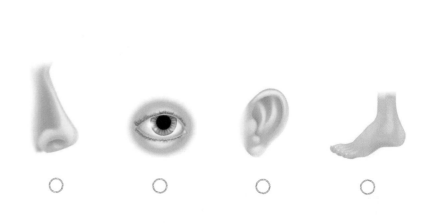

2.

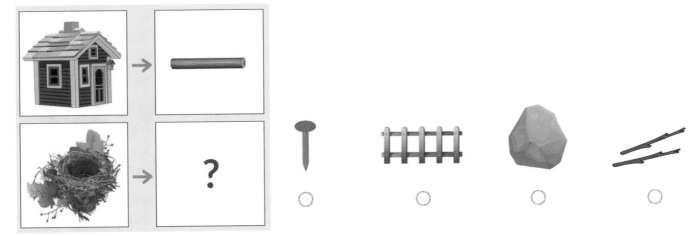

3.

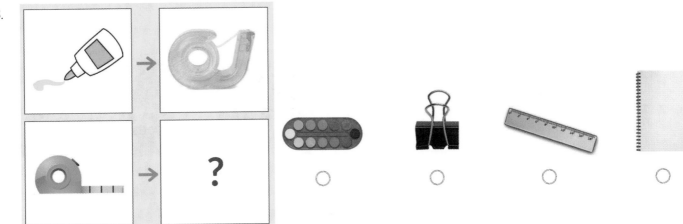

4.

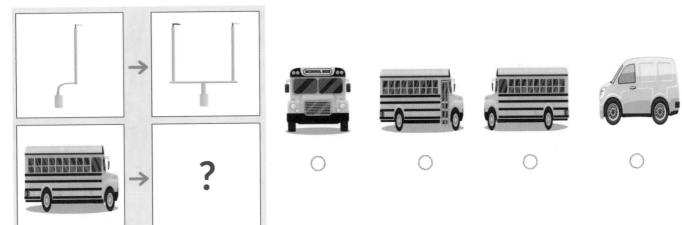

5.

○   ○   ○   ○

6.

○   ○   ○   ○

7.

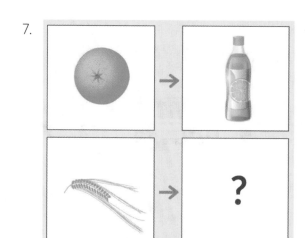

○   ○   ○   ○

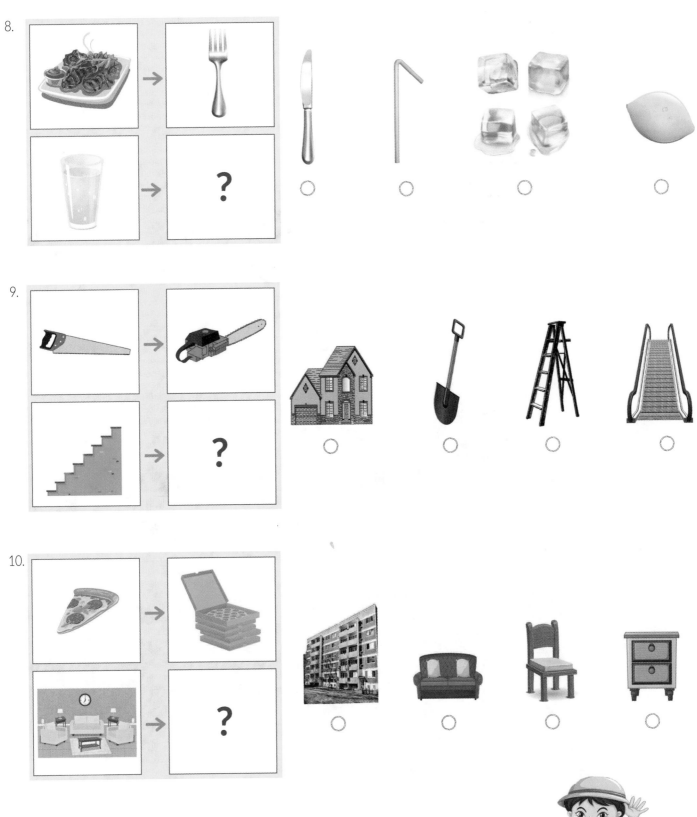

8.

9.

10.

Let's help Anya with the same kind of questions on the next pages, but now we'll use shapes!

Parent Note: As you did with Picture Analogies, together, come up with a "rule" to describe how the top set is related. With Figure Analogies, often this rule will describe how the picture in the left box "changes" into the picture in the right box.

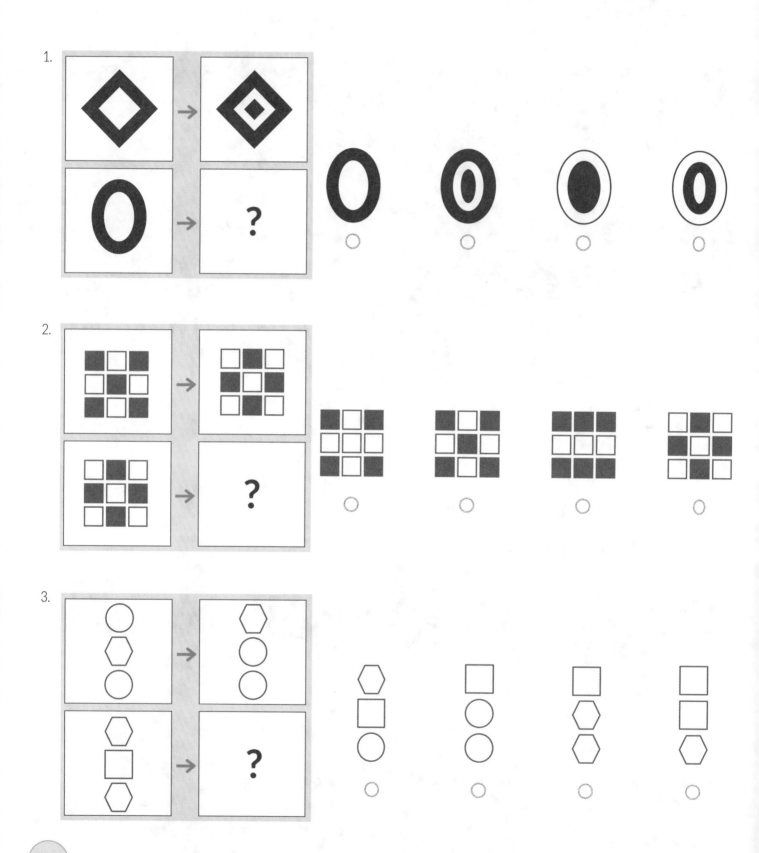

1.

2.

3.

4.

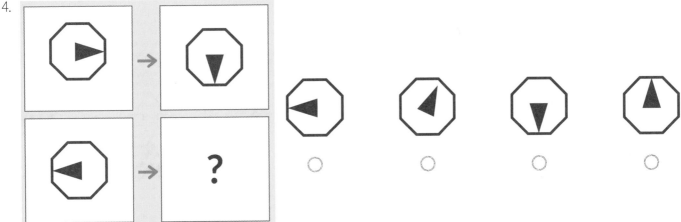

5.

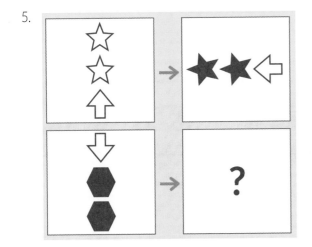

(A)

(B)

(C)

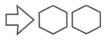
(D)

6.

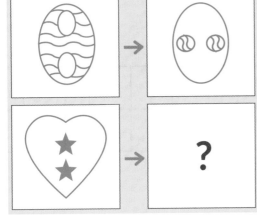

7.

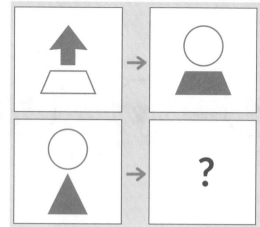    

8.

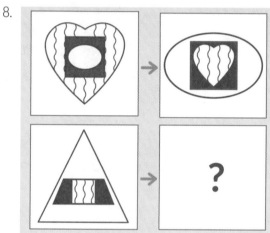  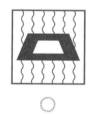  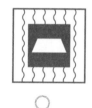

9.

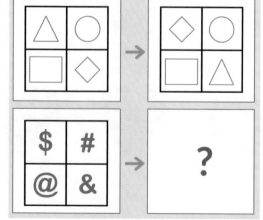      

10.

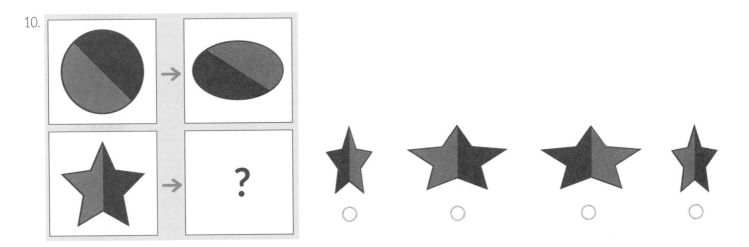

11.

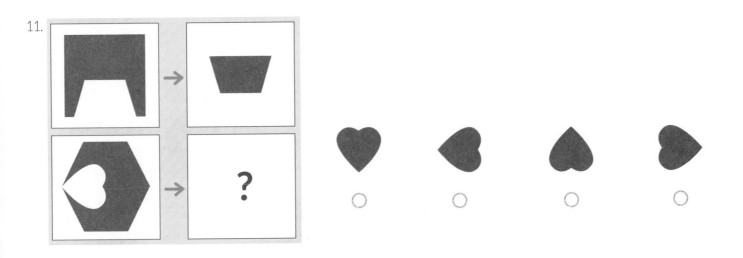

12.

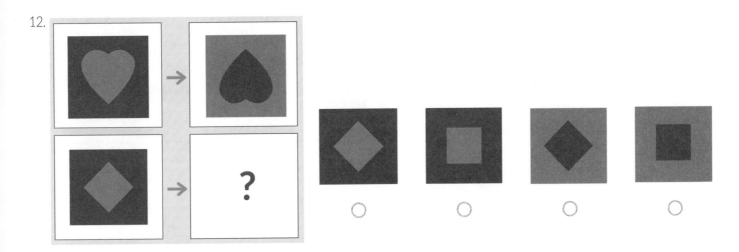

LET'S HELP SOPHIE SOLVE THESE PUZZLES.

Directions: Look at the top row of pictures. These pictures are alike in a certain way. Then, look at the pictures that are on the bottom row. Which picture that is in the bottom row would go best with the pictures that are in the top row?

Example (read this to your child): In the top row, we see a long coat, gloves, and a fuzzy hat. Let's come up with a "rule" to describe how they each are alike. Let's look at them carefully. These are all cold weather clothing that would help keep you warm. Let's look at the bottom row. We need to find the answer choice on the bottom row that follows the same rule. We see shorts, a t-shirt, a sweater, and a tank top. Which one of these goes best with the pictures in the top row? The sweater. The sweater is a kind of cold weather clothing that would keep you warm.

Parent note: As with the analogies questions, when your child finds answer choices that do not follow the "rule," (s)he should eliminate them. If your child finds that more than one choice follows the rule, then (s)he should try to come up with a rule that is more specific.

1.

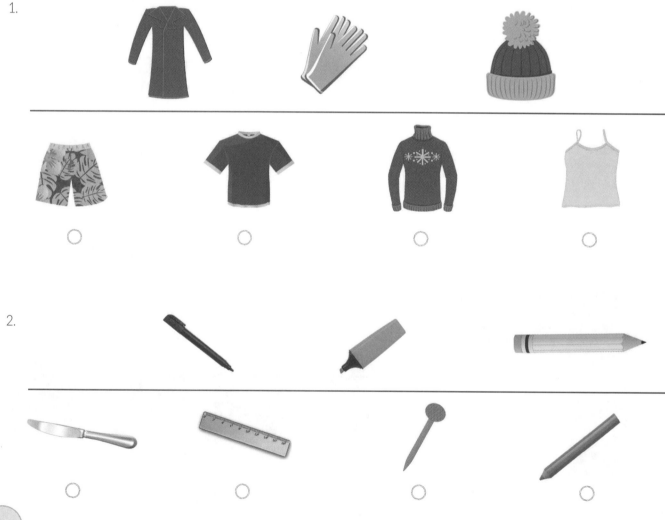

2.

3.

 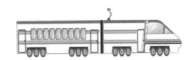 

4.

5.

 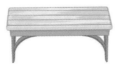 

6.

○ ○ ○ ○

7.

○ ○ ○ ○

8.

○ ○ ○ ○

9.

○　　　　　○　　　　　○　　　　　○

10.

○　　　　　○　　　　　○　　　　　○

11.

○　　　　　○　　　　　○　　　　　○

12.

○ ○ ○ ○

13.

○ ○ ○ ○

14.

○ ○ ○ ○

15.

○   ○   ○   ○

16.

4	38	102	
23	11	96	103
○	○	○	○

17.

s	t	b	
U	o	d	R
○	○	○	○

18.

W	V	M	
T	u	i	l
○	○	○	○

Let's earn more points and help Sophie - this time using shapes.
Which picture from the bottom row goes best with the pictures in the top row?

1.

2.

3.

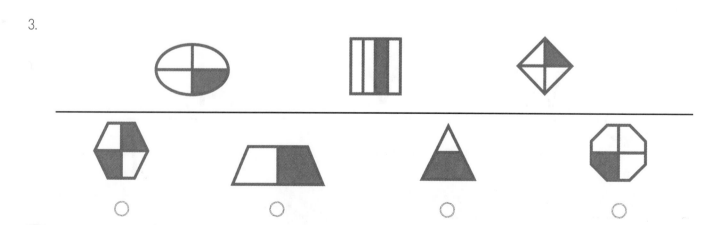

4.

○ ○ ○ ○

5.

  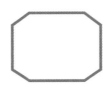

○ ○ ○ ○

6.

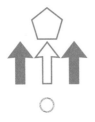  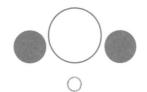 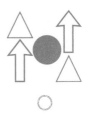

○ ○ ○ ○

7.

  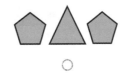 

○ ○ ○ ○

8.

 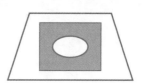

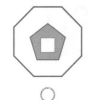 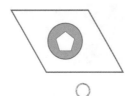 

○   ○   ○   ○

9.

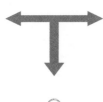 

○   ○   ○   ○

10.

○   ○   ○   ○

11.

○   ○   ○   ○

12.

○ ○ ○ ○

13.

 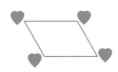

○ ○ ○ ○

14.

   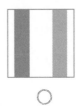

○ ○ ○ ○

15.

○ ○ ○ ○

IT'S TIME TO HELP ALEX ANSWER QUESTIONS AND EARN MORE POINTS!

Directions: Listen to the question and then choose your answer.

Parent Note: These exercises help prepare your child for the Sentence Completion section of the COGAT®. Try to read each question only one time to your child so that (s)he can practice listening skills.

1. Max is going somewhere with a tropical climate. Which one of these will he most likely see?

2. If Sophie wanted to increase the temperature of her soup, which one of these should she use?

3. Which choice shows a circle at the end, a triangle in the middle, and does not have a square ?

4. Which one of these tools would not be used to observe the weather?

5. Anya wants to be a race car driver someday. Which of these should she use to keep her the most secure?

6. Which one of these areas would have the largest population of people?

7. Which choice has a sun in between a cloud and a tree , where the tree is to the right of a sun?

8. Which item would magnify an object the most?

○   ○   ○   ○

9. The driver of which of the below vehicles would have the most experience with emergencies?

○   ○   ○   ○

10. Your friend Max read a book about a fierce animal. Which picture shows what Max's book would have been about?

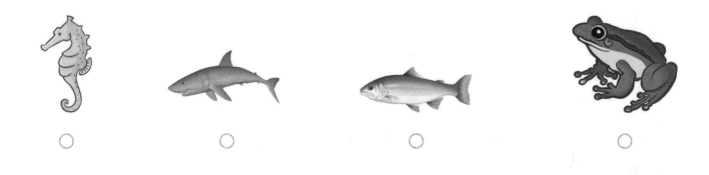

○   ○   ○   ○

11. This afternoon Sophie did only 3 things: she played volleyball, wrote a letter, and ate soup. Which choice shows all of the things Sophie would have used this afternoon?

○   ○   ○   ○

12. If you wanted to prevent a thief from stealing valuables, which of the below would be the best to use?

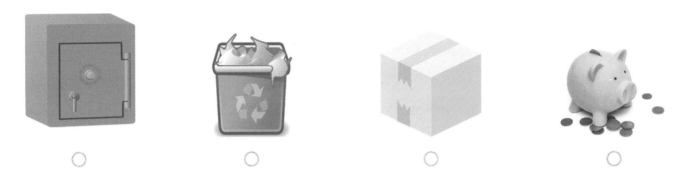

○   ○   ○   ○

13. Max needs to find something that is not made of rubber. Which picture shows what Max needs to find?

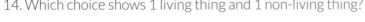

○   ○   ○   ○

14. Which choice shows 1 living thing and 1 non-living thing?

○   ○   ○   ○

15. Which choice has the letter "L" in between the letter "E" and the letter "Z", where the letter "Z" is to the right of the letter "L"?

FEZL   ELZF   ZLFE   LZEF

○   ○   ○   ○

LET'S GIVE ALEX A HAND!

Directions: Look at the top row of pictures. These show a sheet of paper, how it was folded, and how holes were made in the folded sheet of paper. Look at these pictures that are on the bottom row. Which picture shows how the paper would look after the paper is unfolded?

Parent note: To help your child better understand these exercises, demonstrate using real paper and a hole puncher (or scissors). Be sure to point out: the placement of the holes and the number of holes you make in the paper.

On page <u>33</u>, be sure to point out the different sizes of the holes.

1.

2.

3.

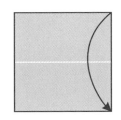 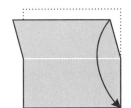 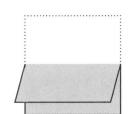 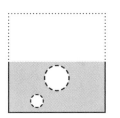

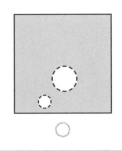 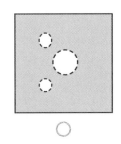 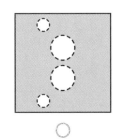 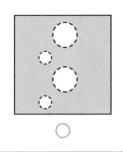

 ○   ○   ○   ○

4.

  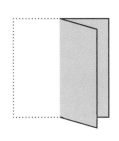 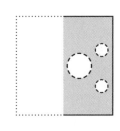

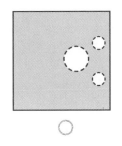 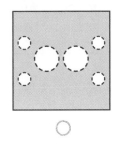 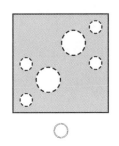 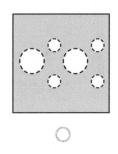

 ○   ○   ○   ○

5.

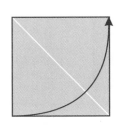 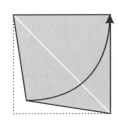 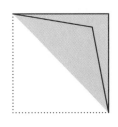 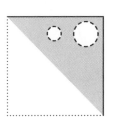

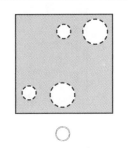 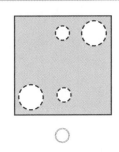 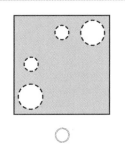 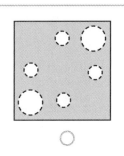

 ○   ○   ○   ○

Directions: Which picture shows how the paper would look after the paper is unfolded?

Important Notes: Make sure your child pays attention to:

- the direction the shapes are pointing
- how the paper is folded
- how many times the paper is folded (i.e., note the difference in #6 and #7)

On page 35 the scissors simply show that the paper was cut.

6.

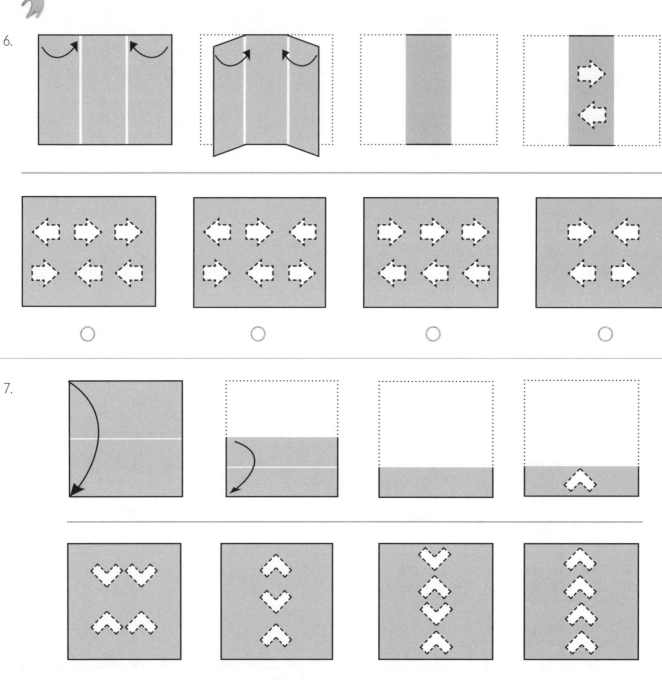

7.

8.

9.

10.

11.

○   ○   ○   ○

12.

○   ○   ○   ○

13.

○   ○   ○   ○

14.

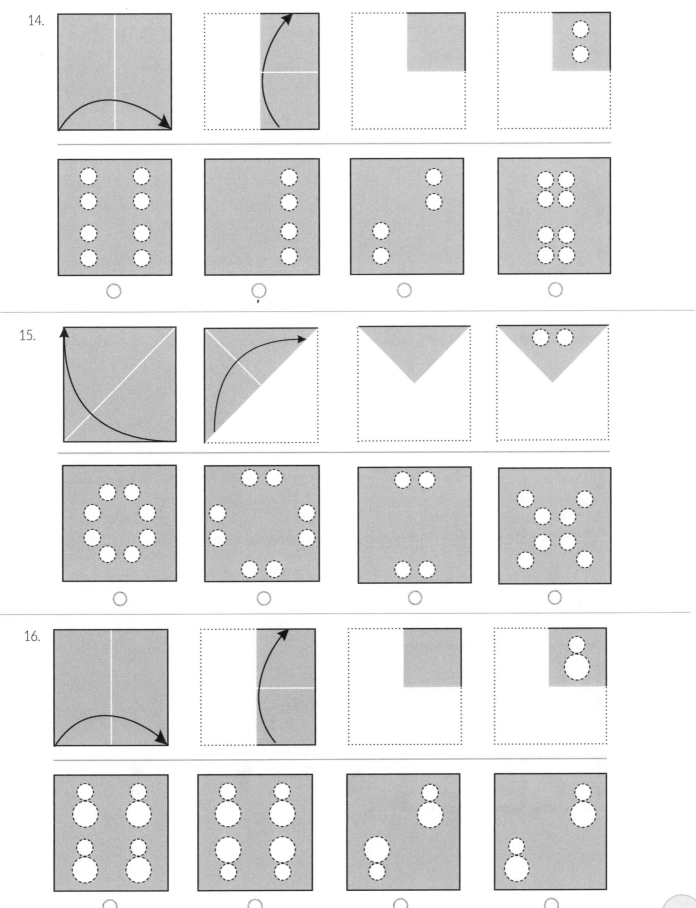

LET'S GIVE MAX A HAND WITH NUMBER PUZZLES.

Section explanation: In this section, the final rod of the abacus is missing. Before the missing rod, the rods of the abacus have a pattern. Have your child look closely at these to determine the pattern. (S)he will then need to select which rod would finish the pattern. Make sure your child carefully and correctly counts the number of abacus beads. Note that some answer choices do not have any beads. This equals "0". The thin gray lines appear in questions that contain rods with more than 5 beads. The thin gray line appears above the 5th bead (or where the 5th bead would be) to facilitate counting.

Due to the complexity of this question type, we have included detailed directions for the first question.

Directions for first question: Here's an abacus. The "circles" on the abacus are beads. These beads are on rods. The beads in the first five rods have made a pattern. Look at the last rod on the abacus. The beads on this rod are missing.

Next to the abacus are four rods. These are the answer choices. Choose which rod would go in the place of the last rod in order to complete the pattern.

Let's look at the abacus. We see 6 beads, then 6 beads, then 1 bead, then 1 bead, then 0 beads. Do you see a pattern? There are 2 rods with 6 beads each, followed by 2 rods with 1 bead each. There is a pair of rods with the same number of beads (6), followed by a different pair of rods with the same number of beads (1). What would go after the rod with 0 beads? The last rod on the abacus is missing. What rod goes here to finish the pattern? (Look at each answer choice.) It is the rod with 0 beads.

Directions for the rest: Which rod would go in the place of the missing rod to finish the pattern?

1.

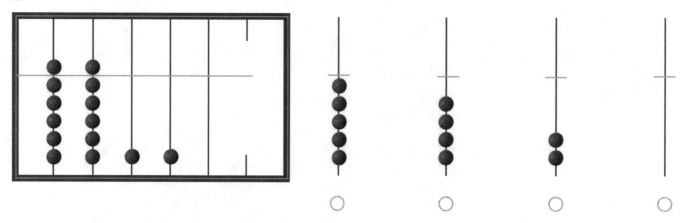

2.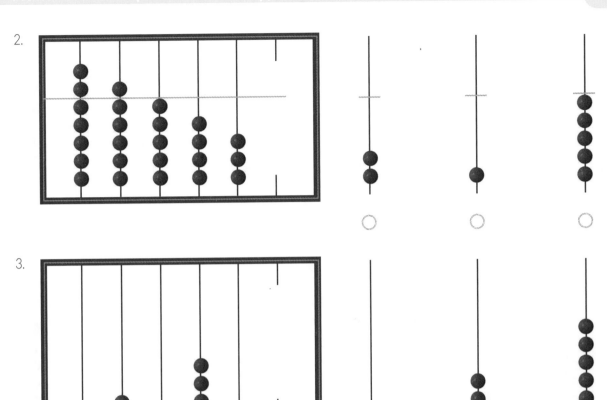

3.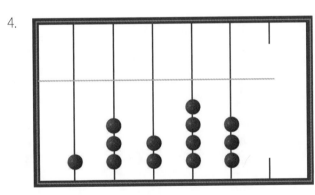

4.

5.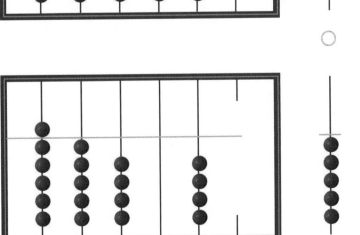

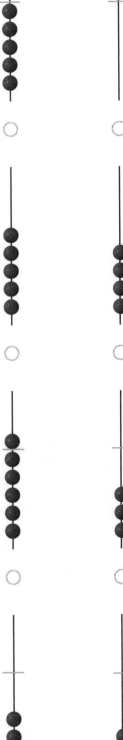

6.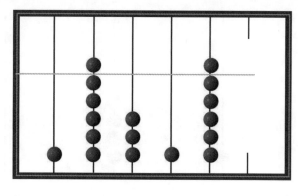

○   ○   ○   ○

7.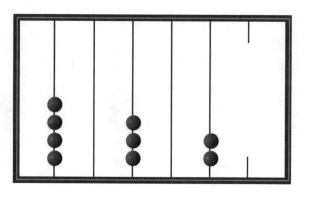

○   ○   ○   ○

8.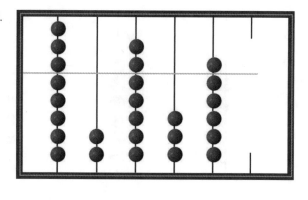

○   ○   ○   ○

9.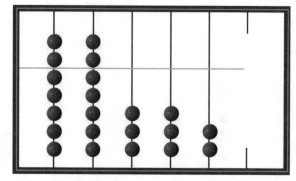

○   ○   ○   ○

MAY NEEDS YOUR HELP WITH MORE NUMBER GAMES!

Directions: Look at the box that has the question mark. Which number would go here so that both of the sides of this equal sign (point to the equal sign) would have the same amount?

Parent Note: Some exercises require three numbers to be added/subtracted. In these, be sure your child correctly distinguishes between the addition and subtraction signs and completes the entire exercise before selecting an answer.

1.

$$9 = 4 + ?$$

4 ○   5 ○   6 ○   7 ○

2.

$$7 = 10 - ?$$

7 ○   5 ○   3 ○   1 ○

3.

$$2 = 10 - 4 - ?$$

1 ○   2 ○   3 ○   4 ○

4.

$$12 = 6 + 6 + ?$$

0 ○   1 ○   2 ○   3 ○

5.

$$11 = 9 + 5 - ?$$

4 ○   3 ○   2 ○   1 ○

6.

$$2 = 12 + 0 - ?$$

8 ○   9 ○   10 ○   11 ○

7.
$9 = 12 + 6 - ?$ 3 4 5 9

8.
$7 = 7 + 6 - ?$ 3 4 5 6

9.
$5 = 11 + 3 - ?$ 7 8 9 0

10.
$0 = 12 - 3 - ?$ 9 8 7 6

11.
$8 = 3 + 12 - ?$ 6 7 8 9

12.
$5 = 9 - 3 - ?$ 0 1 2 3

13.
$12 = 9 + 2 + ?$ 5 4 3 1

14.
$10 = 10 - 0 - ?$ 1 2 3 0

15.
$7 = 11 - 8 + ?$ 0 2 4 8

16.
$0 = 5 + 4 - ?$ 0 9 5 4

17.
$2 = 12 - 4 - ?$ 6 4 8 2

18.
$3 = 10 + 1 - ?$ 0 9 8 7

19.
$1 = 6 + 4 - ?$ 1 2 8 9

20.
$2 = 7 + 3 - ?$ 8 2 3 4

21.
$10 = 12 - 1 - ?$ 1 2 3 4

22.
$5 = 10 - 6 + ?$ 4 3 2 1

23.
3 = 19 - 10 - ?   1 9 6 7
○ ○ ○ ○

24.
2 = 12 - 9 - ?   0 1 3 5
○ ○ ○ ○

25.
8 = 12 - 4 - ?   1 8 0 4
○ ○ ○ ○

26.
5 = 10 - 5 - ?   5 7 1 0
○ ○ ○ ○

27.
2 = 18 - 7 - ?   9 2 0 4
○ ○ ○ ○

28.
12 = 4 + 3 + ?   7 5 3 12
○ ○ ○ ○

29.
8 = 15 + 4 - ?   10 8 9 11
○ ○ ○ ○

30.
3 = 19 - 4 - ?   1 9 12 11
○ ○ ○ ○

31.
9 = 18 - 7 - ?   2 3 11 0
○ ○ ○ ○

32.
2 = 15 - 4 - ?   8 9 2 11
○ ○ ○ ○

33.
12 = 1 + 2 + ?   6 7 8 9
○ ○ ○ ○

34.
1 = 17 - 8 - ?   8 9 7 11
○ ○ ○ ○

35.
9 = 12 - 11 + ?   7 8 9 0
○ ○ ○ ○

36.
3 = 18 - 4 - ?   14 2 11 4
○ ○ ○ ○

37.
8 = 14 - 8 + ?   1 2 4 6
○ ○ ○ ○

38.
3 = 19 - 10 - ?   0 2 6 8
○ ○ ○ ○

WILL YOU HELP MAY SOLVE THESE?

Section explanation: Number analogies questions are similar to the other analogies earlier in this book. Here, however, the top set of boxes and the bottom set of boxes must have the same type of quantitative relationship. Your child must figure out which one of the answer choices would go in the empty box with the question mark to complete the mathematical analogy. Due to the complexity of this section, we have included detailed directions for the first question.

Directions for first question: The top boxes belong together in some way. Look at the top box on the left - there are 7 apples. Look at the top box on the right - there are 10 apples. What has changed between the picture on the left and the picture on the right? We need to come up with a "rule" to describe what has happened. The right box has 3 more things in it than the left box. Three apples were added to get the number of apples in the right box.

Next, let's look carefully at the boxes in the bottom row. The first box has 4 strawberries. The second box is empty. Look carefully at the row of pictures next to the boxes. Which one of these goes in the empty box? The answer is "7 strawberries." This is 3 strawberries more than the left box. On the bottom row, the last choice has 7 strawberries.

Directions for the rest: Which answer choice would go inside the empty box at the bottom?

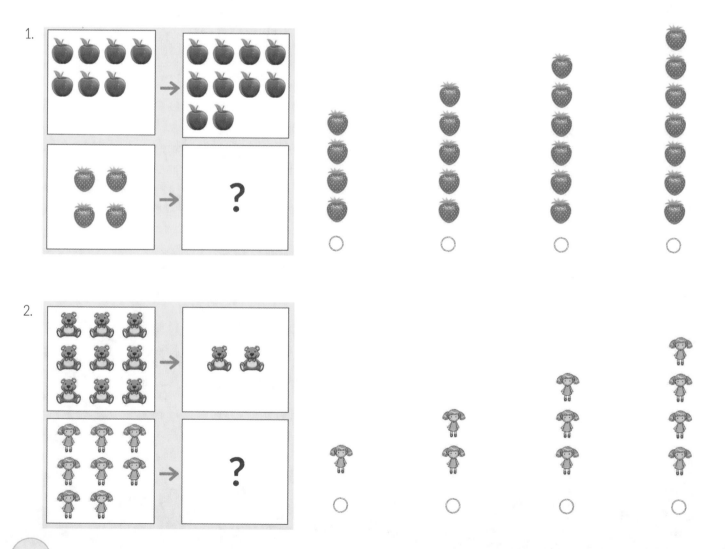

3.

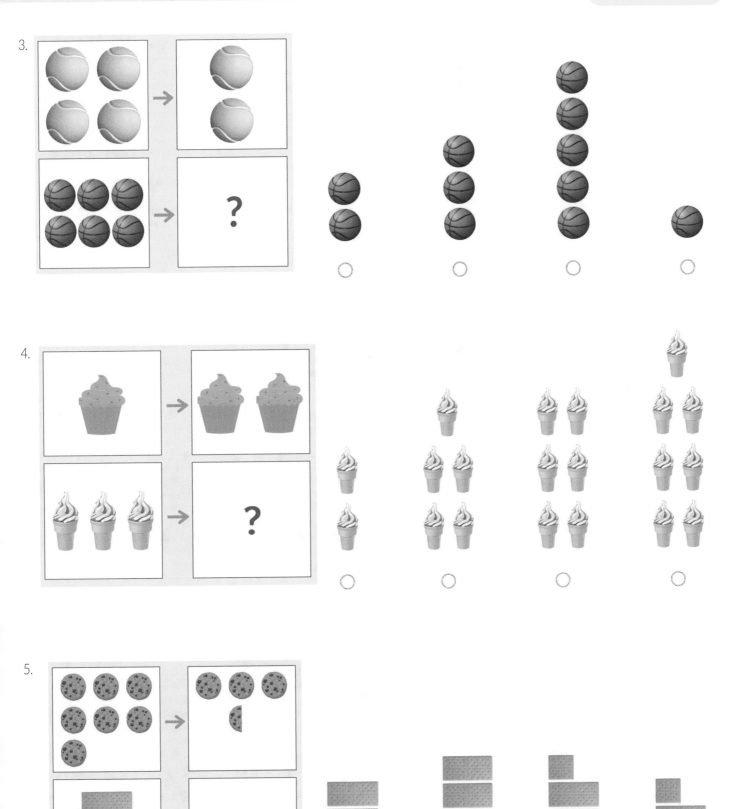

4.

5.

6.

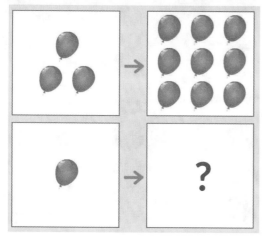

Ⓐ

Ⓑ

Ⓒ

Ⓓ

7.

Ⓐ

Ⓑ

Ⓒ

Ⓓ

8.

Ⓐ

Ⓑ

Ⓒ

Ⓓ

9.

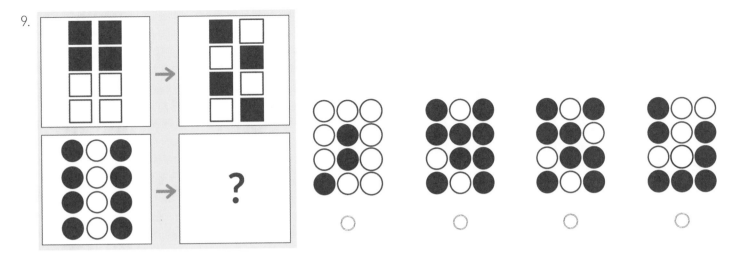

10.

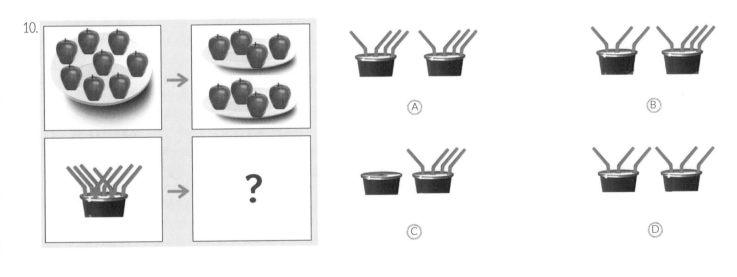

11.

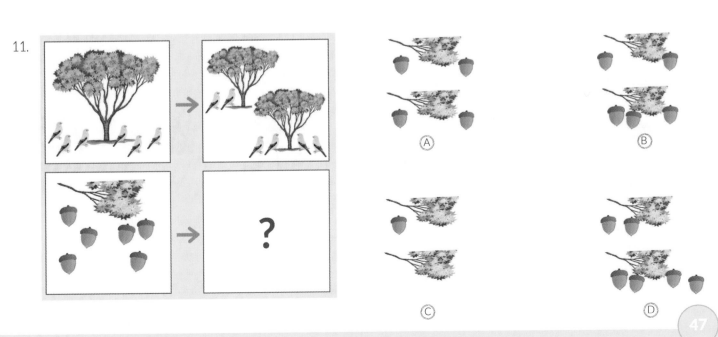

12.

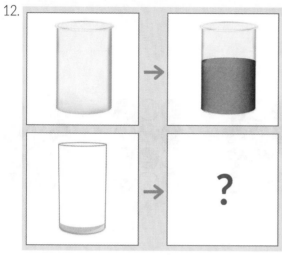    

13.

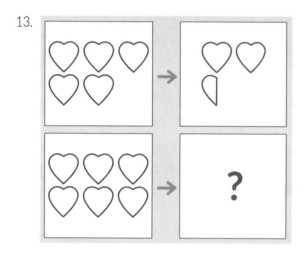    

14.

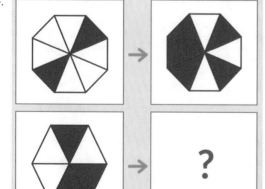    

PRACTICE QUESTION SET INSTRUCTIONS

Reading Directions: Tell your child to listen carefully, because you can read the directions to him/her only one time. (Test administrators often read directions only once.)

Test instructors will not let your child know if his/her answers are correct or not. If you wish for the Practice Question Set to serve as a "practice test," then as your child completes the Practice Question Set, we suggest you do the same. Instead of saying if answers are correct or not, you could say something like, "Nice work, let's try some more."

Navigation Figures: Assuming your child has completed the Workbook, then (s)he is familiar with the exercise format (navigating through pages with rows of questions). To make the test navigation easier for kids, some gifted tests use image markers in place of question numbers and in place of page numbers.

We include the "markers" so that your child can be familiar with them.

When your child needs to look at a new page, you would say, for example, "Find the page where there is an umbrella at the bottom." When your child needs to look at a question, you would say, for example, "Find the row where there is a bug."

These markers are listed on the Directions & Answer Key pages so that you can read them to your child.

The Practice Question Set is divided into three sections, to mirror the different "batteries" of the COGAT®: Verbal Section (pages 50-63), the Quantitative Section (pages 64-77), and the Non-Verbal Section (pages 78-90).

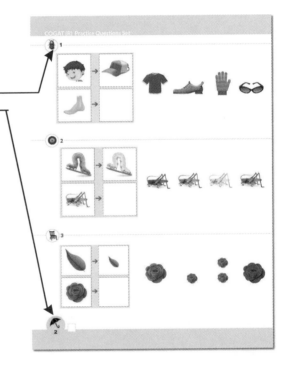

Time: Allow one minute per question, approximately. There are 3 sections (Verbal, Quantitative, Non-Verbal). We suggest doing 1 section per day. However, you may do more should you wish.

Evaluation: The Practice Question Set is labeled by question type. After your child is done, on your own (without your child) go through the Set by question type, writing the number answered correctly in the space provided on the answer key. While these practice questions are not meant to be used in place of an official assessment, these will provide a general overview of strengths/weaknesses, as they pertain to test question type. For questions your child didn't answer correctly, go over the question and answer choices again with him/her. Compare the answer choices, specifically what makes the correct answer choice the right choice. Since gifted programs typically accept only top performers, we encourage additional practice.

We offer additional COGAT® practice books as well as FREE questions in eBook format.
See page 96 and get your free eBook today!

1.

2.

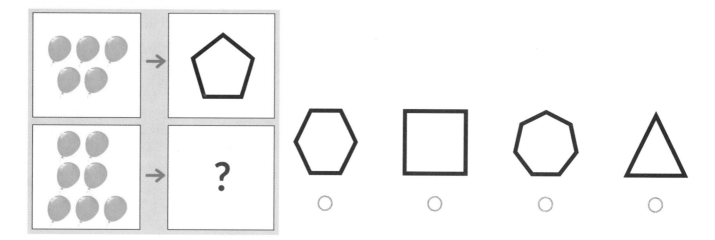

3.

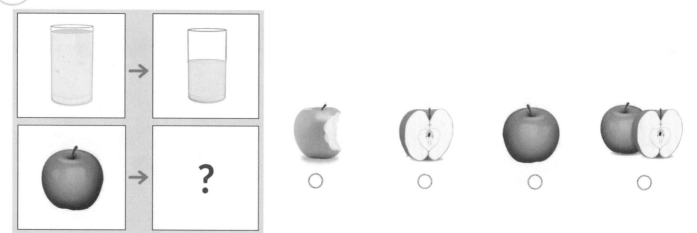

4.

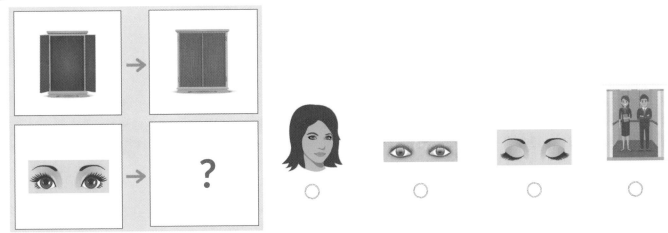

 5.

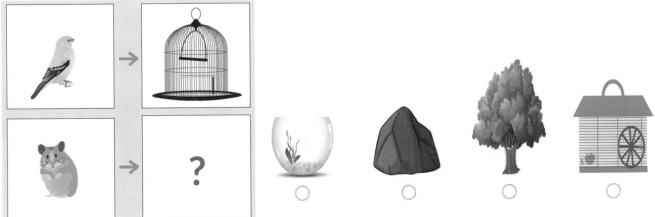

 6.

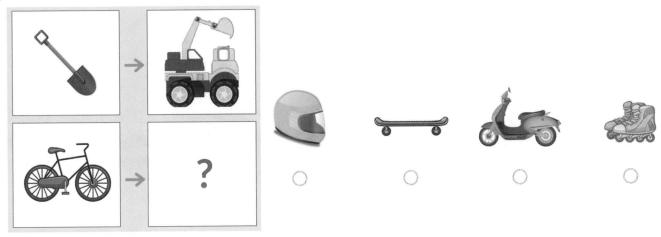

7.

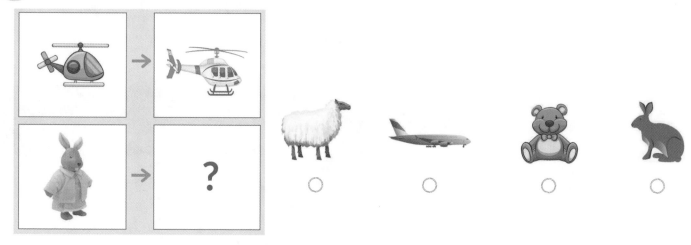

8.

9.

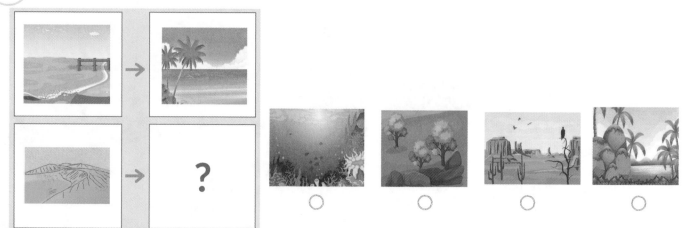

10.

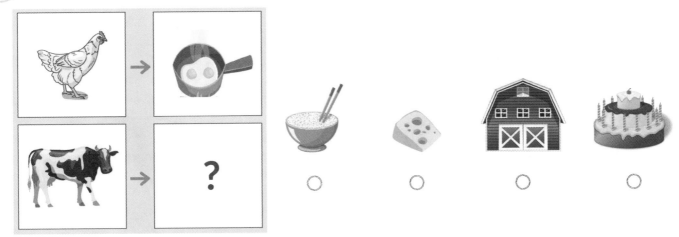

11.

12.

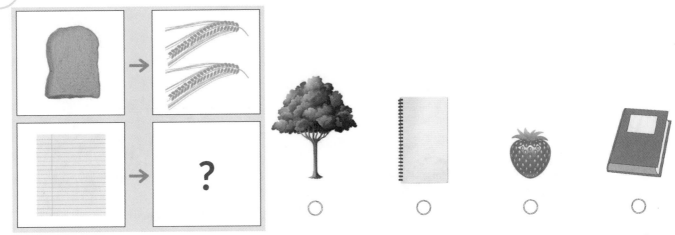

13.

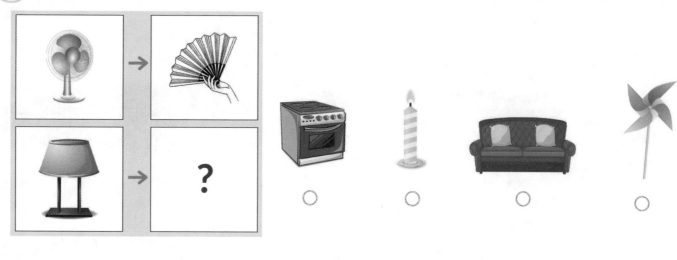

14.

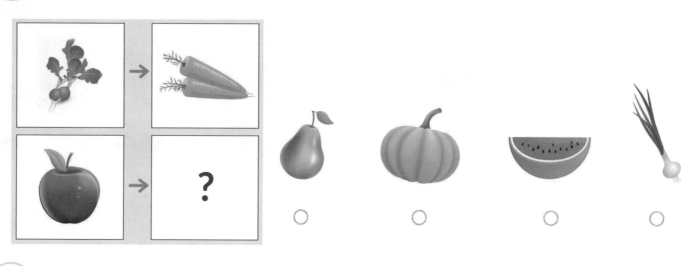

15.

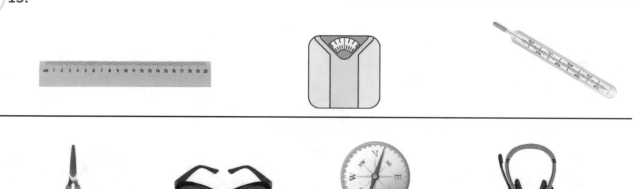

54

16.

○   ○   ○   ○

 17.

 ○   ○   ○   ○

 18.

 ○   ○   ○   ○

19.

U   O   I

W   V   M   E
○   ○   ○   ○

20.

43   1   209

---

0   12   47   308
○   ○   ○   ○

21.

○   ○   ○   ○

22.

 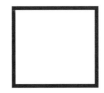 

○ ○ ○ ○

 23.

○ ○ ○ ○

 24.

○ ○ ○ ○

25.

◯ ◯ ◯ ◯

 26.

◯ ◯ ◯ ◯

 **27.**

◯ ◯ ◯ ◯

28.

○ ○ ○ ○

 29.

○ ○ ○ ○

 30.

○ ○ ○ ○

 31.

○ ○ ○ ○

32.

○   ○   ○   ○

 33.

○   ○   ○   ○

 34.

○   ○   ○   ○

 35.

○   ○   ○   ○

36.

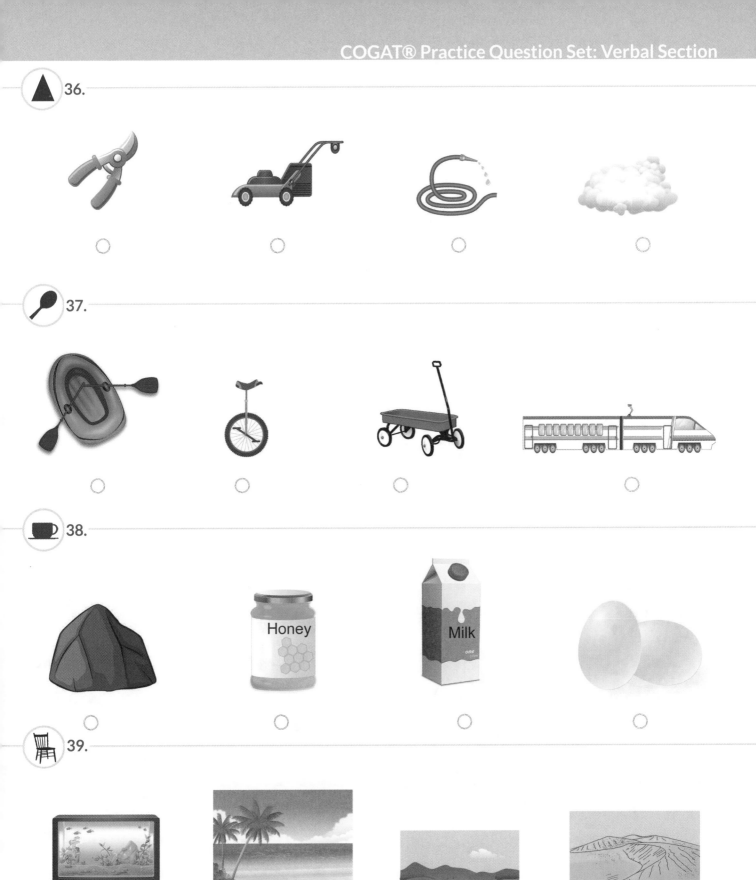

37.

38.

39.

40.

○ ○ ○ ○

 41.

○ ○ ○ ○

 42.

○ ○ ○ ○

 43.

 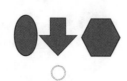  

○ ○ ○ ○

44.

○   ○   ○   ○

 45.

○   ○   ○   ○

 46.

○   ○   ○   ○

 47.

○   ○   ○   ○

48.

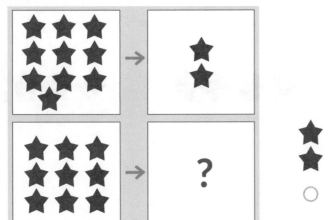

 49.

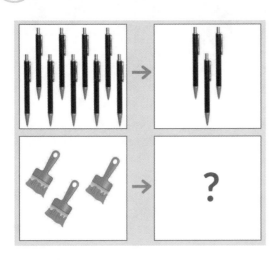

 50.

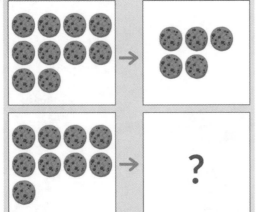

51.

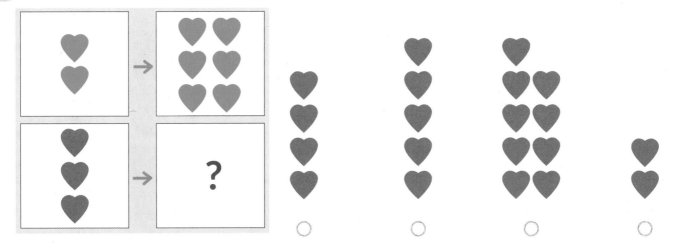

52.

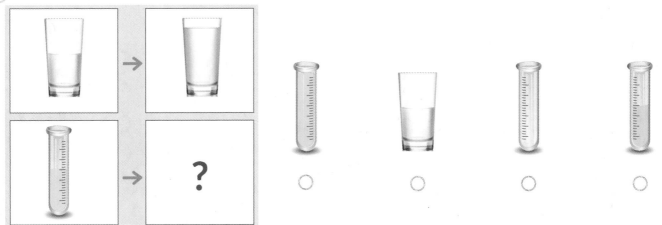

53.

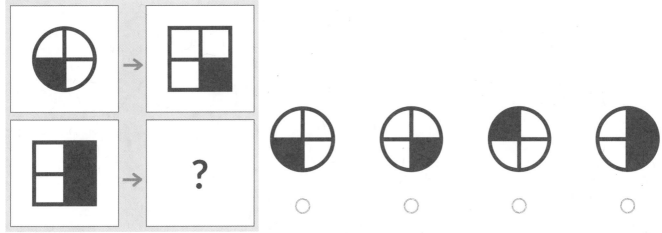

54.

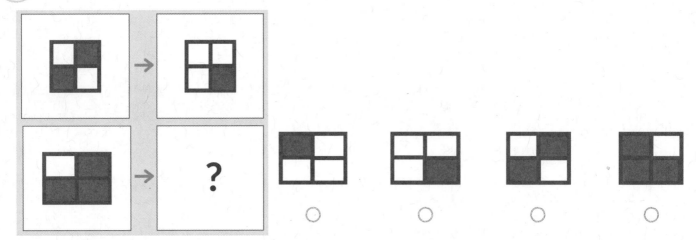

 55.

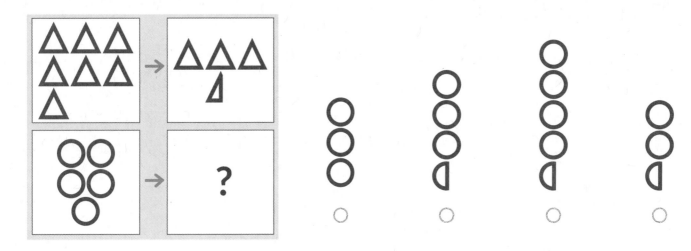

 56.

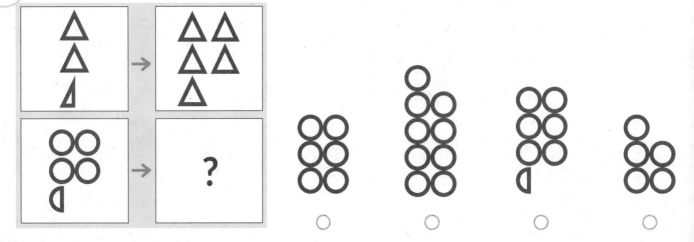

57.

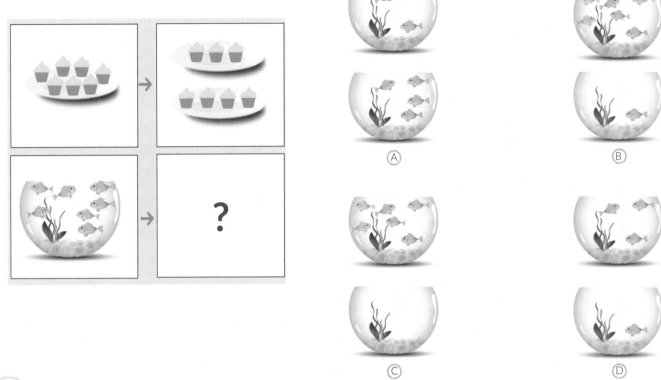

58.

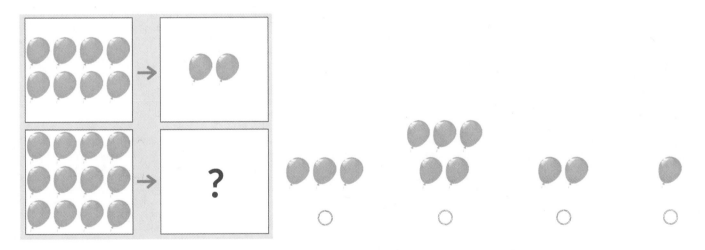

Continue to the next page.

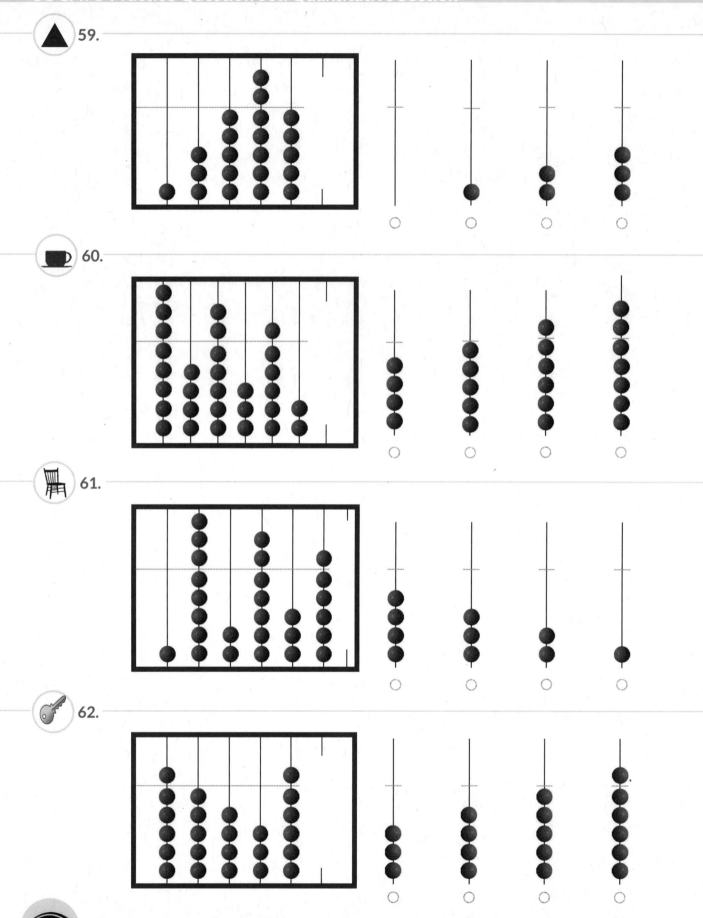

59.

60.

61.

62.

63.

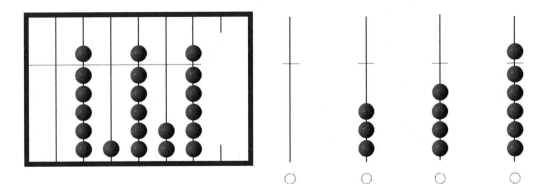

64.

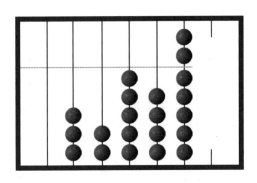   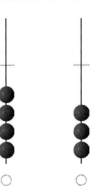

65.

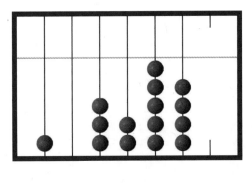   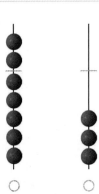

66.

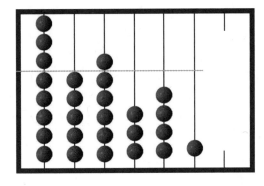   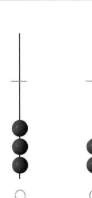

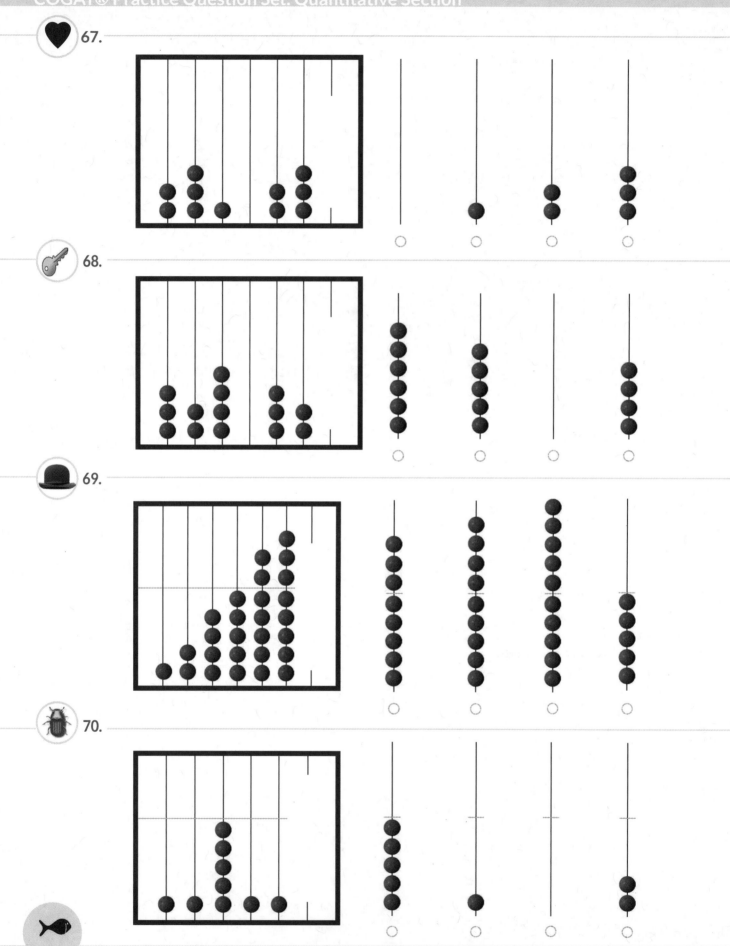

67.

68.

69.

70.

71.

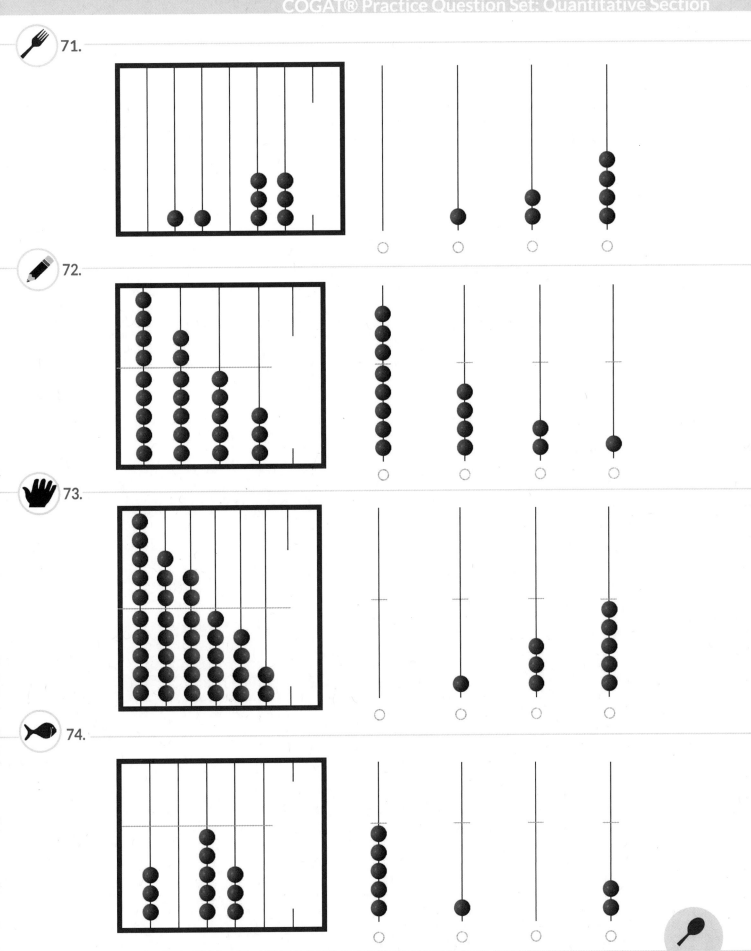

72.

73.

74.

75.

| 6 | = | 12 | + | 3 | - | ? |

7 ○   8 ○   9 ○   10 ○

76.

| 0 | = | 11 | - | 6 | - | ? |

3 ○   4 ○   5 ○   6 ○

77.

| 11 | = | 1 | + | 7 | + | ? |

3 ○   4 ○   5 ○   6 ○

78.

| 9 | = | 0 | + | 9 | - | ? |

3 ○   2 ○   1 ○   0 ○

79.

| 1 | = | 2 | + | 11 | - | ? |

9 ○   10 ○   11 ○   12 ○

80.

| 10 | = | 5 | - | 3 | + | ? |

8 ○   9 ○   10 ○   11 ○

81.

| 4 | = | 12 | + | 3 | - | ? |

12 ○   11 ○   10 ○   9 ○

82.

| 8 | = | 11 | + | 9 | - | ? |

12 ○   13 ○   14 ○   15 ○

83.

| 0 | = | 10 | - | 9 | - | ? |

3 ○   2 ○   1 ○   0 ○

84.

| 12 | = | 4 | - | 2 | + | ? |

10 ○   11 ○   12 ○   0 ○

85.

| 12 | = | 2 | - | 0 | + | ? |

8 ○   9 ○   10 ○   11 ○

86.

| 3 | = | 11 | + | 2 | - | ? |

8 ○   9 ○   10 ○   11 ○

87.

| 5 | = | 3 | + | 11 | - | ? |

10 ○   9 ○   8 ○   7 ○

88.

| 10 | = | 0 | + | 12 | - | ? |

5 ○   4 ○   3 ○   2 ○

89.

| 7 | = | 12 | - | 3 | - | ? |

2 ○   1 ○   0 ○   3 ○

90.

| 12 | = | 11 | - | 9 | + | ? |

9 ○   12 ○   11 ○   10 ○

91.

| 11 | = | 15 | - | 8 | + | ? |

3 ○   4 ○   5 ○   6 ○

92.

| 2 | = | 15 | - | 9 | - | ? |

6 ○   5 ○   4 ○   3 ○

93.

| 0 | = | 14 | - | 7 | - | ? | 7 ○ | 6 ○ | 5 ○ | 4 ○ |

 94.

| 15 | = | 8 | + | 3 | + | ? | 10 ○ | 4 ○ | 5 ○ | 6 ○ |

 95.

| 13 | = | 2 | + | 1 | + | ? | 11 ○ | 12 ○ | 9 ○ | 10 ○ |

 96.

| 1 | = | 15 | - | 13 | - | ? | 1 ○ | 2 ○ | 3 ○ | 4 ○ |

 97.

| 2 | = | 1 | - | 1 | + | ? | 0 ○ | 1 ○ | 2 ○ | 3 ○ |

 98.

| 3 | = | 5 | - | 3 | + | ? | 5 ○ | 1 ○ | 0 ○ | 2 ○ |

75

99.

16 = 14 - 9 + ?

5   12   10   11

100.

4 = 15 - 9 - ?

1   2   3   4

101.

2 = 19 - 6 - ?

11   13   10   9

102.

14 = 17 - 8 + ?

15   9   5   0

103.

18 = 14 - 9 + ?

5   13   12   11

104.

15 = 14 - 8 + ?

6   7   8   9

105.

2 = 19 - 8 - ?   9 ○   11 ○   5 ○   7 ○

106.

1 = 10 + 2 - ?   9 ○   10 ○   11 ○   8 ○

107.

4 = 17 + 2 - ?   15 ○   19 ○   5 ○   16 ○

108.

5 = 15 - 10 - ?   5 ○   0 ○   10 ○   1 ○

109.

14 = 17 - 6 + ?   2 ○   11 ○   8 ○   3 ○

110.

17 = 12 - 9 + ?   3 ○   14 ○   13 ○   15 ○

111.

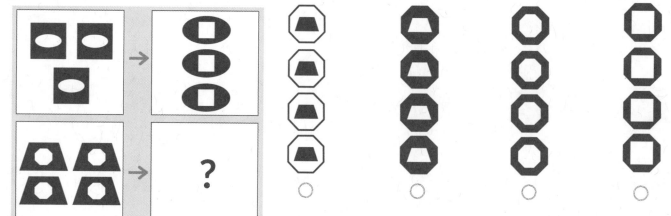

112.

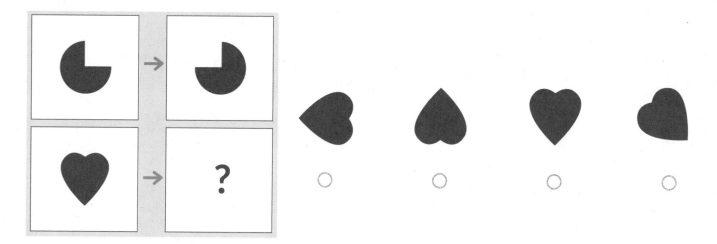

113.

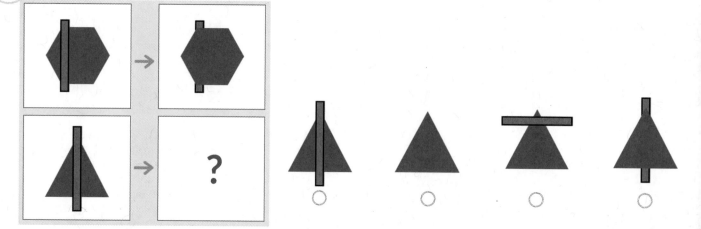

114.

115.

116.

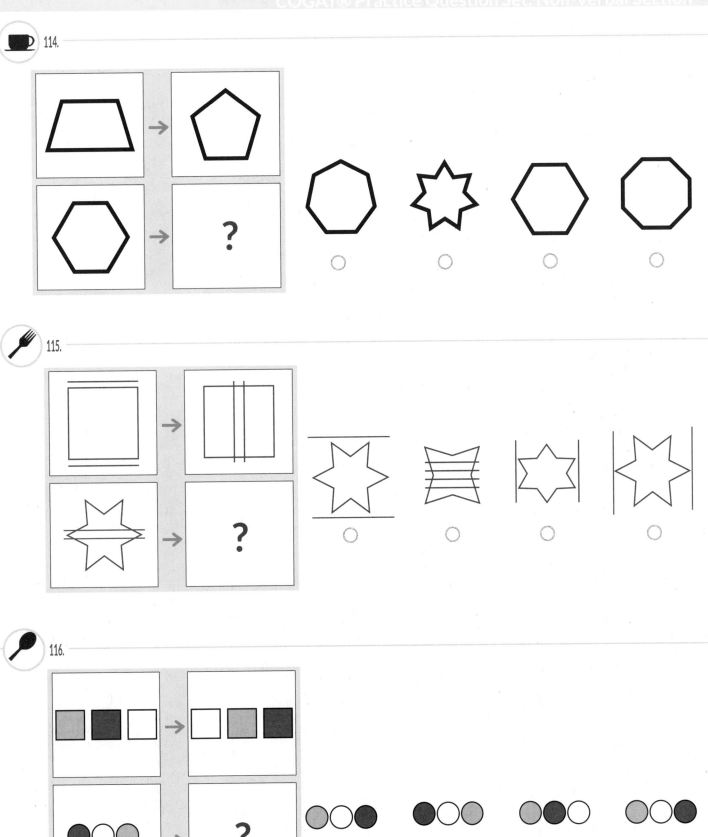

117.

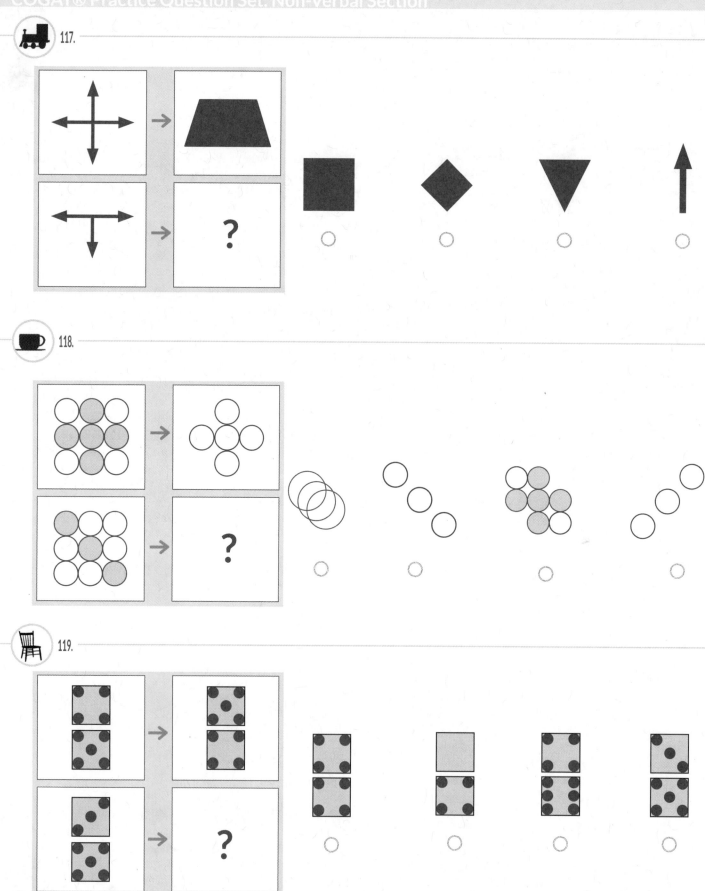

118.

119.

120.

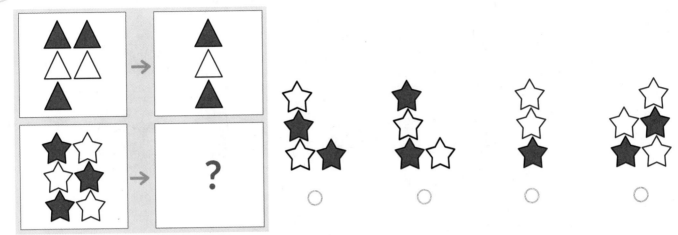

 121.

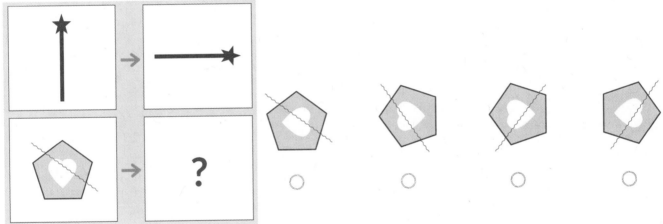

122.

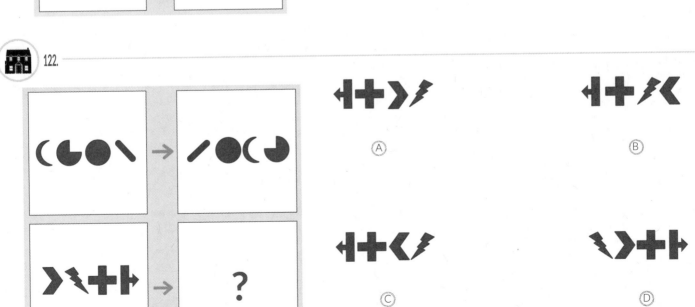

123.

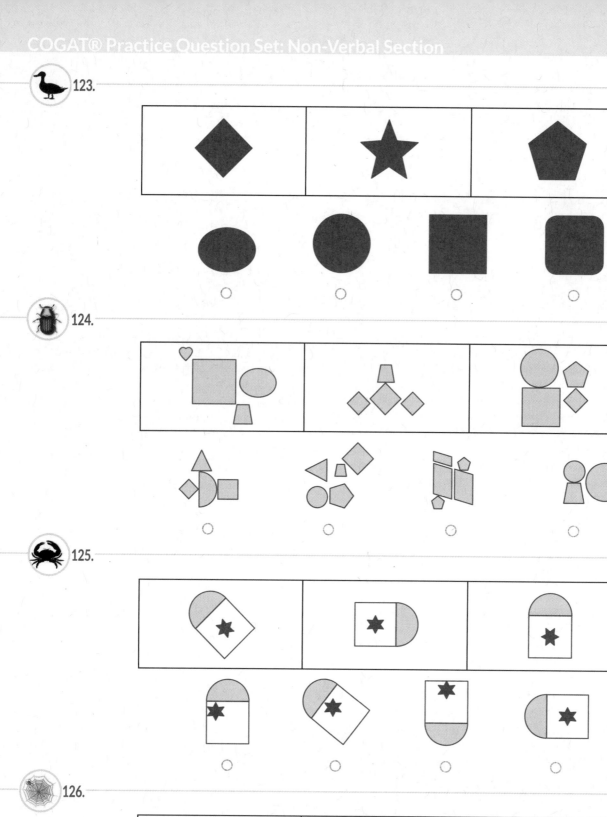

124.

125.

126.

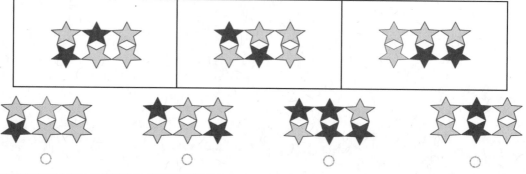

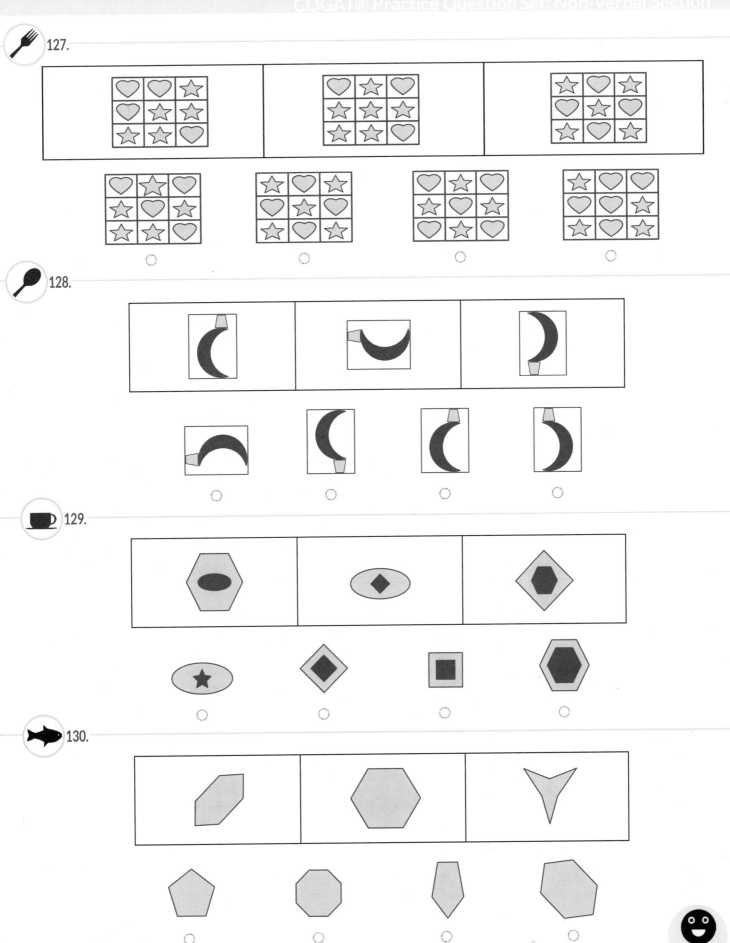

131.

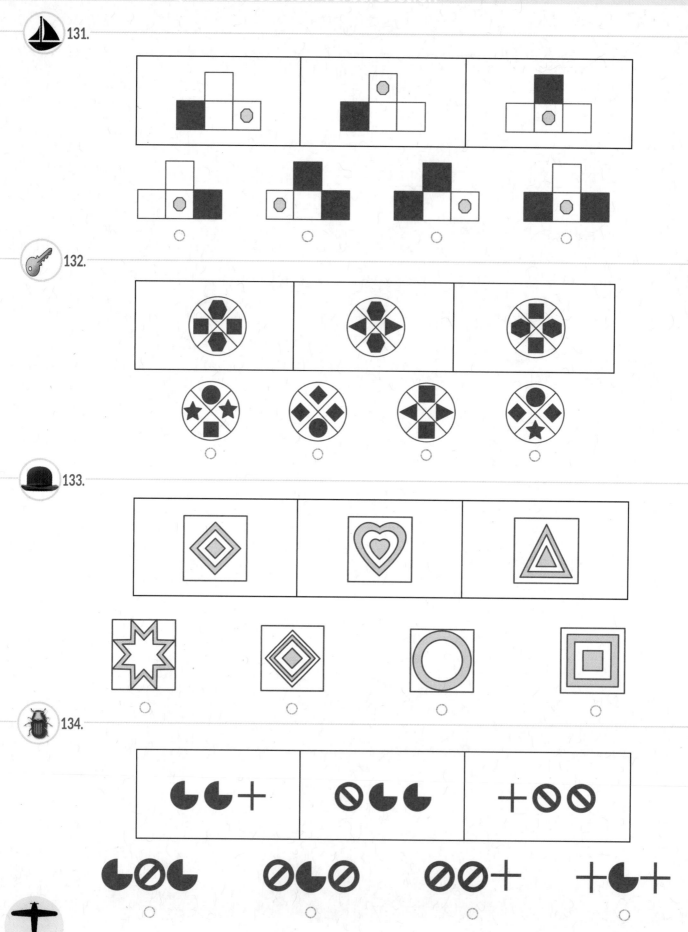

132.

133.

134.

135.

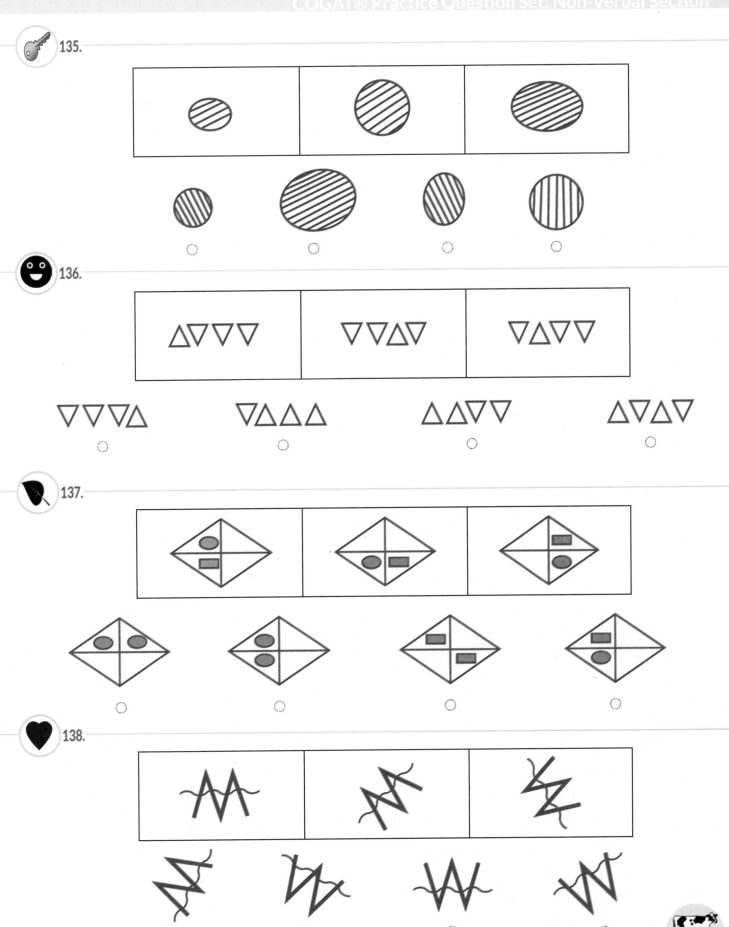

136.

137.

138.

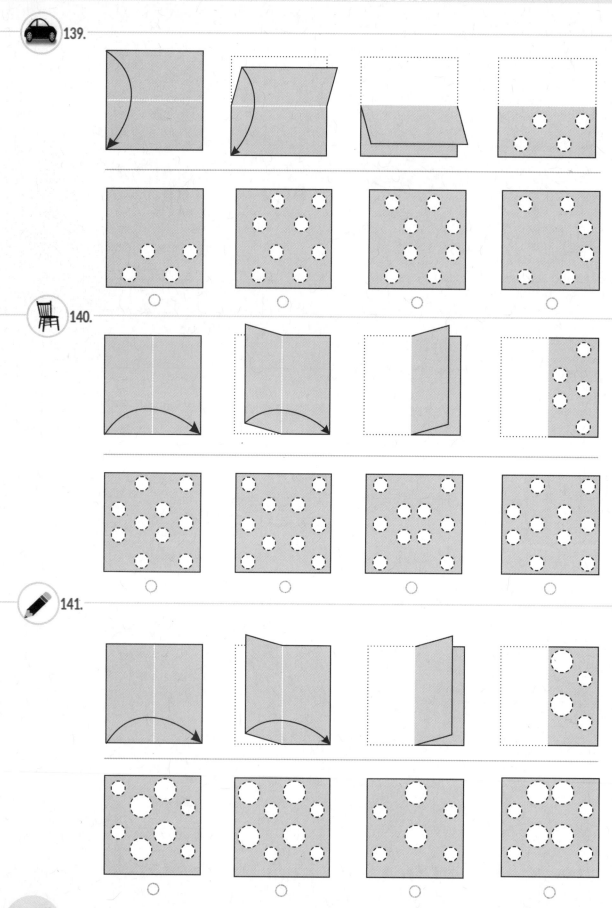

139.

140.

141.

142.

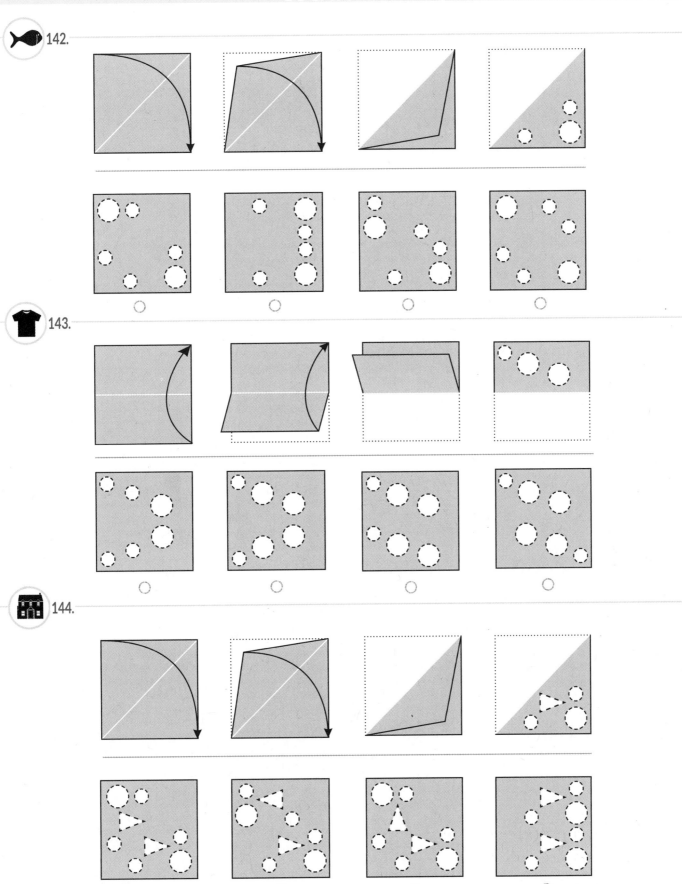

143.

144.

145.

146.

147.

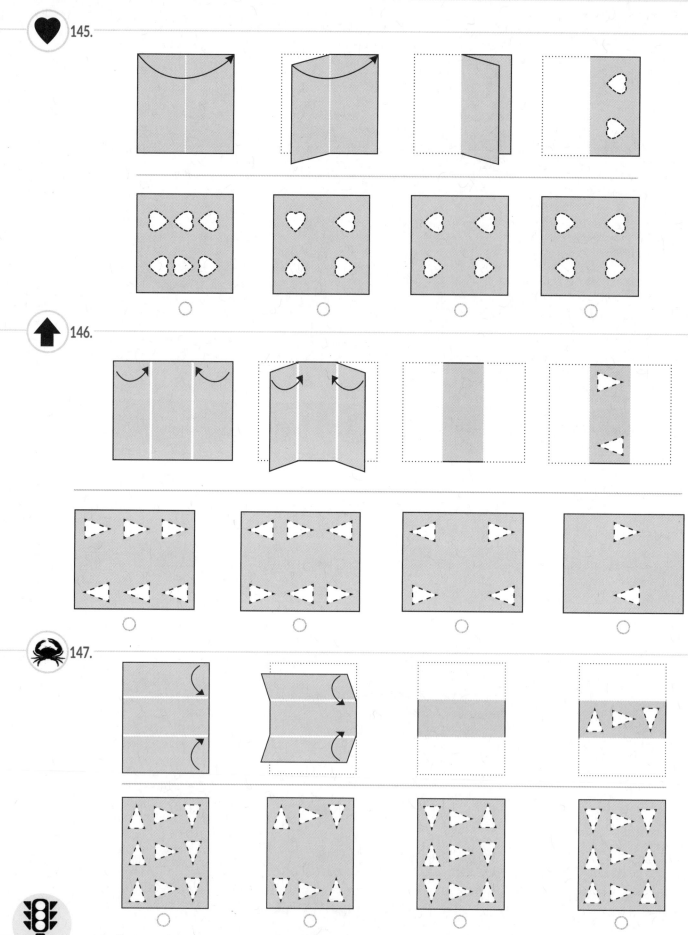

148.

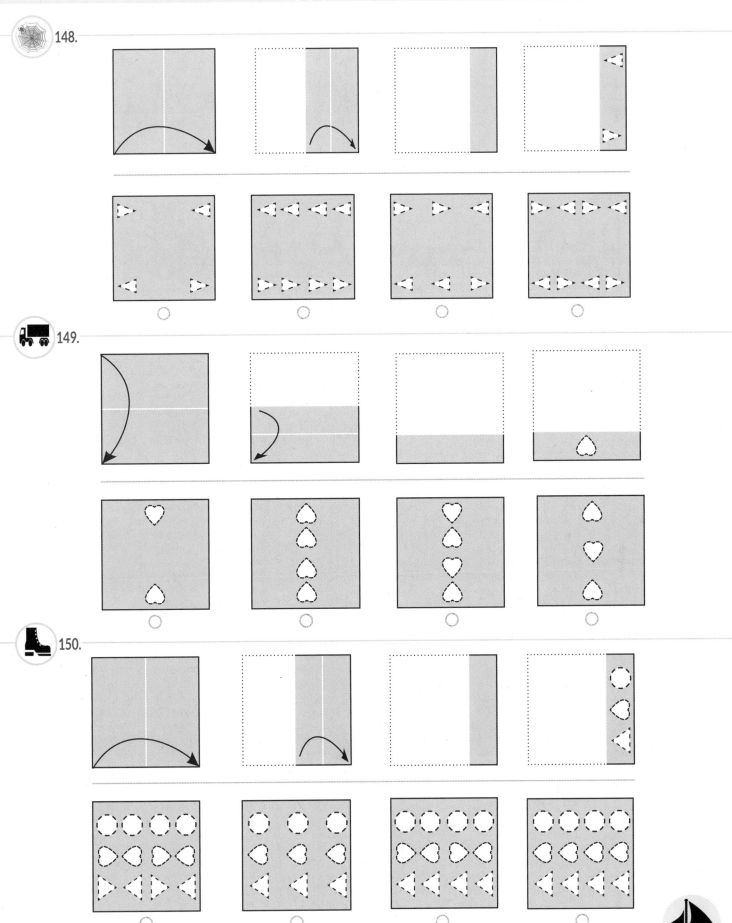

149.

150.

151.

152.

153.

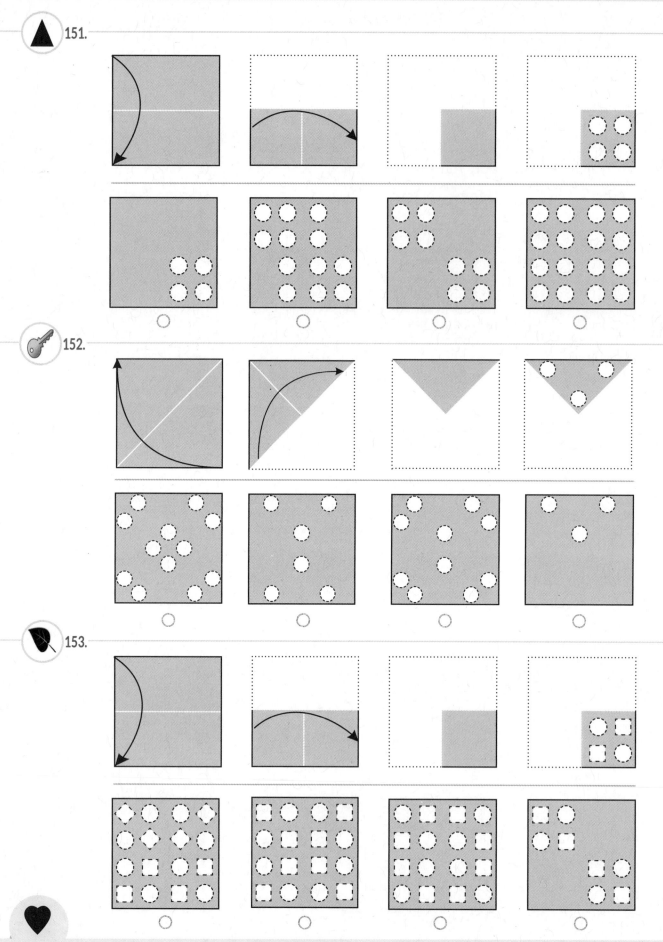

✂ Answer Key For Workbook (p.10-48)

Picture Analogies

1. B
2. D: home > material used to build it (person's home; bird's home)
3. C: item with similar function > item with similar function (holding things together; measuring)
4. A: object turned to side > object facing front
5. B: same type of animal > same type of animal (reptiles; birds)
6. C: animal > animal's habitat
7. C: ingredient > food produced by ingredient (oranges are used to make orange juice; wheat is used to make crackers)
8. B: item > utensil used to consume (eat/drink) item
9. D: objects with similar function, but the objects in the right boxes do the function faster and they are a motorized version of the objects in the left box (a chainsaw cuts much faster than a handsaw, thanks to a motor; an escalator takes you up/down levels faster than steps, thanks to a motor)
10. A: object > multiple versions of this object found together (pizza slice > multiple pizza slices found combined together inside pizza boxes; room in a home > multiple rooms found combined together inside an apartment building)

Figure Analogies

1. B: small version of outside shape added in the middle
2. B: white becomes purple & vice versa; also the top left & bottom right -and- top right & bottom left figures are the same
3. C: in second box, middle shape & top shape switch positions
4. D: shapes rotate clockwise
5. D: group of shapes rotate counterclockwise & the two shapes that are the same change color
6. C: smaller shapes inside larger shape align horizontally and the pattern/color of the smaller shapes and larger shape switch (on first row the wavy lines & white switch; on the second row the red & white switch)
7. B: the bottom shape changes color from white to green on the top row & from green to white on the bottom row; the top shape changes from a green arrow to a white circle on the top row & from a white circle to a green arrow on the bottom row
8. A: the larger outer shape & the smaller inner shape switch positions
9. A: the figures in the top left & bottom right positions switch
10. C: in the right box, the colors of the shape switch & the shape gets shorter/wider
11. D: the right box contains the white shape from the left box & the shape has switched colors and has rotated 180 degrees
12. C: the figures rotate 180 degrees and switch colors (with the diamond in the bottom boxes you would not notice the 180 degree flip the way you do with the heart in the top boxes due to the diamond's shape – the top half mirrors the bottom half)

Picture Classification

1. C
2. D: used to write/draw
3. D: vehicles that carry many people at once
4. A: continents
5. B: made of wood
6. D: fish
7. A: instruments
8. B: holds liquid
9. C: provides heat/cooks food
10. D: has lens(es)
11. C: cold items
12. D: sweets
13. A: have wheels
14. B: animal homes
15. D: checkered designs
16. C: even numbers
17. C: lowercase consonants
18. A: uppercase consonants

Figure Classification

1. B: same color
2. C: shapes divided in half
3. D: ¼ filled
4. A: 3 shapes filled
5. B: 8-sided shapes
6. C: group of 3 shapes
7. D: 2 of the same shape next to each other
8. D: small oval in middle
9. B: 4 arrow points
10. B: 1 circle filled
11. A: dotted line at same position on arrow
12. B: 1 large octagon, 1 small cross, 1 small triangle
13. D: larger shape & smaller shapes opposite colors
14. A: 1 light green bar & 2 dark green bars in square
15. D: 2 small shapes on either side with 1 larger version of the same shape in middle

Sentence Completion

1. B (tropical bird)
2. D (microwave)
3. C
4. A (a thermometer to measure body temperature)
5. A (helmet)
6. A (city)
7. D
8. D (microscope)
9. B (police)
10. B (shark)
11. C
12. A
13. D (rock)
14. D (tree & eggshell)
15. B

Paper Folding

1. D	2. A	3. C	4. B	5. C	6. B	7. C
8. C	9. B	10. D	11. D	12. C	13. A	14. A
15. B	16. B					

Number Series (Abacus Activity)

1. D
2. A: with each rod, -1
3. C: 0-1-0-3-0-5; every other rod is 0 & between these '0' rods, the # of beads increases +2
4. B: rods 1, 3, 5 increase by 1; rods 2, 4, 6 increase by 1
5. A: 6-5-4-0-4-5
6. C: 1-6-3-1-6-3
7. A: rods 1, 3, 5 decrease by 1; rods 2, 4, 6 have "0"
8. A: rods 1, 3, 5 decrease by 1; rods 2, 4, 6 increase by 1
9. C: 7-7-3-3-2-2

Number Puzzles:

1. B	2. C	3. D	4. A	5. B
6. C	7. D	8. D	9. C	10. A	11. B	12. B
13. D	14. D	15. C	16. B	17. A	18. C	19. D
20. A	21. A	22. D	23. C	24. B	25. C	26. D
27. A	28. B	29. D	30. C	31. A	32. B	33. D
34. A	35. B	36. C	37. B	38. C		

Number Analogies

1. D
2. A (-7)
3. B (1/2)
4. C (mult. by 2)
5. D (1/2)
6. A (mult. by 3)
7. D (mult. by 4)
8. A (one-quarter / div. by 4)
9. C (same number of shapes dark blue/ white)
10. A (the first box has 8 things (apples or straws); the second box has these same 8 objects divided equally, 4 & 4)
11. D (the first box has 6 items (birds/acorns); the second box has these same 6 items, but they are split 2 & 4)
12. B (both just over half filled)
13. C (half)
14. D (+3 filled/-3 white)

COGAT® PRACTICE QUESTION SET: DIRECTIONS & ANSWER KEY

-Be sure to read 'Practice Question Set Instructions' first (page 49).

-This answer key is divided into charts according to COGAT® question type so that you can easily see how your child performs on each of the test's nine question types. Each chart includes the directions you will read to your child. It also lists the page navigation icons and question navigation icons that you will read to your child to assist with navigation.

1) If turning to a new page, say to your child: "Find the page where there is a(n) ___ at the bottom." (These sentences are listed in each chart in *italics*.)

2) Next, say to your child: "Find the row where there is a(n) __. " (These are the question navigation icons listed in the first column. They are underlined.)

3) Then, read the directions to your child. These are in the gray box. Each question type has the same directions for the questions of that question type. The only exception is the Sentence Completion questions on p.93. In the Sentence Completion chart, the directions are in the chart's third column and not in a gray box.

COGAT® QUESTION TYPE 1: PICTURE ANALOGIES (VERBAL SECTION)

Directions for all Picture Analogy questions: Look at these boxes that are on top. The pictures that are inside belong together in some way. Then, look at these boxes that are on the bottom. One of these boxes on the bottom is empty. Look next to the boxes. There is a row of pictures. Which one would go together with this picture that is in the bottom box like these pictures that are in the top boxes?

"Find the row where there is a(n) _____."	Question Number	Answer	Child's Answer
(p. 50) "Find the page where there is an umbrella at the bottom."			
(Help child find the page where questions start.)			
Sun	1	A: baby version	
Fish	2	C: balloon # > shape with # of sides	
Key	3	B: half	
(p. 51) "Find the page where there is a pair of glasses at the bottom."			
Car	4	C: open > closed	
Web	5	D: animal > animal's enclosed home	
Truck	6	C: similar function, but motorized & faster	
(p. 52) "Find the page where there is a train at the bottom."			
Star	7	D: toy version > real version	
Chair	8	B: # of dots on dice = # of legs animal has	
Crab	9	C: similar environment	
(p. 53) "Find the page where there is a ball at the bottom."			
Black Rectangle	10	B: food made from this animal	
Fork	11	D: 1 > many grouped together	
Spoon	12	A: bread is made from wheat; paper from trees	
(p. 54) "Find the page where there is a bird at the bottom."			
Hat	13	B: similar function, without electricity	
Cup	14	A: root produce > tree produce	

Picture Analogy Questions Answered Correctly: _____ out of 14

COGAT® QUESTION TYPE 2: PICTURE CLASSIFICATION (VERBAL SECTION)

Directions for all Picture Classification questions: Look at the top row of pictures. These pictures are alike in a certain way. Then, look at the pictures that are on the bottom row. Which picture that is in the bottom row would go best with the pictures that are in the top row?

"Find the row where there is a(n) _____."	Question Number	Answer	Child's Answer
Heart	15	C: used to measure	
(p. 55) "Find the page where there is a house at the bottom."			
Stoplight	16	B: pretend people	
Car	17	A: dairy products	
Key	18	B: insects	
(p. 56) "Find the page where there is a triangle at the bottom."			
Boat	19	D: uppercase vowels	
Sun	20	C: odd numbers	
Chair	21	D: half is showing	
(p. 57) "Find the page where there is a boot at the bottom."			
Arrow	22	A: 3's (tricycle has 3 wheels)	

COGAT® QUESTION TYPE 2: PICTURE CLASSIFICATION, CONTINUED (VERBAL SECTION)

"Find the row where there is a(n) _____."	Question Number	Answer	Child's Answer
Web	23	B: holds paper together	
Truck	24	D: grows on trees	
(p. 58) *"Find the page where there is a beetle at the bottom."*			
Shirt	25	C: extinct/prehistoric animals	
Ant	26	A: toy animals	
Chair	27	D: has spots	

Picture Classification Questions Answered Correctly: _____ out of 13

COGAT® QUESTION TYPE 3: SENTENCE COMPLETION (VERBAL SECTION)

"Find the row where there is a(n)____."	Question Number	Directions (Say to child)	Answer	Child's Answer
(p. 59) *"Find the page where there is a key at the bottom."*				
Tree	28	Which one of these would be used to measure time?	C	
Triangle	29	At least once a week Anna participates in a surgery. Which of these pictures most likely is Anna?	A	
Shoe	30	Which food does not require removing a shell before eating?	C	
Duck	31	Which one cannot be used to produce a form of electricity?	D	
(p. 60) *"Find the page where there is a hammer at the bottom."*				
Truck	32	Which ingredient is the most common in bakery products?	B	
Crab	33	John harvests crops and raises animals. Which one is he?	C	
Web	34	Which choice shows a vegetable that is a root and a fruit that grows on a vine?	A	
Fork	35	Which of these is least likely to prevent a sports injury?	B	
(p. 61) *"Find the page where there is a leaf at the bottom."*				
Triangle	36	Alex visits a garden. He puts his hand on the ground and it feels damp. What object could have been recently used in the garden?	C	
Spoon	37	Max must arrive quickly to a destination, which is over 100 miles away. Which form of transportation should he choose?	D	
Cup	38	Which one of these does not have to do with bees, cows, or chickens?	A	
Chair	39	Which location would be the most affected by a tsunami?	B	
(p. 62) *"Find the page where there is a black rectangle at the bottom."*				
Star	40	Which animal would have more legs than a dog?	C (insects have 6)	
Car	41	Today Anya did 3 things. She practiced a musical instrument, played tennis, and helped her mother take measurements for building a table. Which picture shows all of the things Anya used today?	B	
Shirt	42	Which choice shows 2 animals that live on land and 1 animal that lives on both land and water?	A	
Stoplight	43	Which choice shows an arrow in the middle, a hexagon at the end, and does not have an oval?	D	
(p. 63) *"Find the page where there is a duck at the bottom."*				
Key	44	Which choice has the diamond to the right of a circle, where the circle is in between a rectangle and the diamond?	C	
Hat	45	Which choice shows 2 foods that grow on trees and 2 foods that grow under the ground?	A	
Fork	46	For an art project Alex needs 3 things: something to write with, something to cut with, and something to hold things together. Which picture shows the 3 things Alex needs?	D	
Spoon	47	Freddie has 2 favorite animals: 1 that swims and 1 that cannot fly. Which picture shows Freddie's 2 favorite animals?	B	

Sentence Completion Questions Answered Correctly: _____ out of 20

COGAT® QUESTION TYPE 4: NUMBER ANALOGIES (QUANTITATIVE SECTION)

"Find the row where there is a(n) _____."	Question Number	Answer	Child's Answer
Directions for all Number Analogy questions: The pictures inside the top boxes belong together in some way. Look at the bottom boxes. One box is empty. Which answer choice would go together with the bottom picture like these pictures on top?			
(p. 64) *"Find the page where there is a butterfly at the bottom."*			
Bike	48	B (-8)	
Key	49	A (divide by 3)	
Crab	50	D (half)	

"Find the row where there is a(n) _____."	Question Number	Answer	Child's Answer
(p. 65) *"Find the page where there is a flower at the bottom."*			
Car	51	C (multiply by 3)	
Fork	52	A (half full > almost full)	
Spoon	53	D (same # of white parts/same # of blue parts)	
(p. 66) *"Find the page where there is a black arrow at the bottom."*			
Star	54	C (-1 filled section -or- +1 white section)	
Ant	55	D (half)	
Crab	56	B (multiply by 2)	
(p. 67) *"Find the page where there is a shirt at the bottom."*			
Stoplight	57	A (7 items > 7 items split into 3 & 4)	
Fork	58	A (divide by 4)	

Number Analogies Questions Answered Correctly: _____ out of 11

COGAT® QUESTION TYPE 5: NUMBER SERIES - ABACUS (QUANTITATIVE SECTION)

Directions for all Number Series questions: Here's an abacus. The beads on the first rods have made a pattern. Look at the last rod on the abacus. The beads on this rod are missing. Next to the abacus are four rods. These are the answer choices. Choose which rod would go in the place of the last rod in order to complete the pattern.

"Find the row where there is a(n) _____."	Question Number	Answer	Child's Answer
(p. 68) *"Find the page where there is an eye at the bottom."*			
Triangle	59	D (1-3-5-7-5-3)	
Cup	60	B (rods 1,3,5,7 decrease by 1; 2,4,6 decrease by 1)	
Chair	61	A (rods 1,3,5,7 increase by 1; 2,4,6 decrease by 1)	
Key	62	C (6-5-4-3-6-5)	
(p. 69) *"Find the page where there is a bike at the bottom."*			
Boat	63	B (rods 1,3,5,7 increase by 1; rods 2,4,6 = 6)	
Arrow	64	A (rods 1,3,5,7 increase by 2; 2,4,6 increase by 2)	
Cup	65	C (rods 1,3,5,7 increase by 2; 2,4,6 increase by 2)	
Stoplight	66	D (rods 1,3,5,7 decrease by 2; 2,4,6 decrease by 2)	
(p. 70) *"Find the page where there is a fish at the bottom."*			
Heart	67	B (2-3-1-0-2-3-1)	
Key	68	D (3-2-4-0-3-2-4)	
Hat	69	C (+1, +2, +1, +2, +1, +2; 8 beads +2 = 10 beads)	
Bug	70	A (1-1-5-1-1-5)	
(p. 71) *"Find the page where there is a spoon at the bottom."*			
Fork	71	A (0-1-1-0-3-3-0; 0-same-same-0-same-same-0)	
Pencil	72	D (each rod decreases by 2)	
Hand	73	B (rods decrease in pattern: -2,-1,-2,-1,-2,-1)	
Fish	74	A (3-0-5-3-0-5)	

Number Series Questions Answered Correctly: _____ out of 16

COGAT® QUESTION TYPE 6: MATH PUZZLES - EQUATIONS (QUANTITATIVE SECTION)

Directions for all Math Puzzles questions: Look at the box that has the question mark. Which number would go here so that both of the sides of this equal sign would have the same amount?

"Find the row with a(n) ___."	Question Number	Answer	Child's Answer	"Find the row with a(n) ___."	Question Number	Answer	Child's Answer	"Find the row with a(n) ___."	Question Number	Answer	Child's Answer
(p. 72) *"Find the page with a table at the bottom."*				(p. 74) *"Find the page with a crab at the bottom."*				(p. 76) *"Find the page with a cup at the bottom."*			
Pencil	75	C		Pencil	87	B		Umbrella	99	D	
Star	76	C		Star	88	D		House	100	B	
Crab	77	A		Sun	89	A		Crab	101	A	
Web	78	D		Key	90	D		Boat	102	C	
Fork	79	D		Fork	91	B		Triangle	103	B	
Spoon	80	A		Spoon	92	C		Truck	104	D	
(p. 73) *"Find the page with a hand at the bottom."*				(p. 75) *"Find the page with a fish at the bottom."*				(p. 77) *"Find the page with a sun at the bottom."*			
Shirt	81	B		Black Rectangle	93	A		Arrow	105	A	
Fish	82	A		Chair	94	B		Boot	106	C	
Bug	83	C		Ball	95	D		Leaf	107	A	
Car	84	A		Train	96	A		Hammer	108	B	
Tree	85	C		Heart	97	C		Butterfly	109	D	
Truck	86	C		Bird	98	B		Flower	110	B	

Math Puzzles Questions Answered Correctly: _____ out of 36

COGAT® QUESTION TYPE 7: FIGURE ANALOGIES (NON-VERBAL SECTION)

Directions for all Figure Analogy questions: The pictures inside the top boxes belong together in some way. Look at these boxes that are on the bottom. One of these boxes on the bottom is empty. Look next to the boxes. There is a row of pictures. Which one would go together with this picture that is in the bottom box like these pictures that are in the top boxes?

"Find the row with a(n) ___.	Question	Answer	Child's Answer
(p. 78) *"Find the page where there is an ant at the bottom."*			
Pencil	111	B: inside/outside shapes switch color & position, then align vertically	
Stoplight	112	C: flips; due to shape of hearts, hearts appear the same	
Crab	113	D: lighter blue bar goes behind larger shape	
(p. 79) *"Find the page where there is a hat at the bottom."*			
Cup	114	A: from left to right box, the shape has +1 side	
Fork	115	D: on top, 2 lines come together & rotate 90°; on bottom, they separate & rotate 90° (the opposite of the top)	
Spoon	116	C: turquoise becomes white, dark blue becomes turquoise, white becomes dark blue -OR- the 3rd shape becomes the 1st and the remaining shapes move to the 2nd and 3rd positions in the same order	
(p. 80) *"Find the page where there is a wheel at the bottom.*			
Train	117	C: # of arrow points = # of shape sides	
Cup	118	B: position of blue circles in 1st box = position & quantity of white circles in second box	
Chair	119	A: top dice +1, bottom dice -1	
(p. 81) *"Find the page where there is a fish at the bottom."*			
Cow	120	B: -2 shapes from the second column	
Boat	121	D: shape group rotates 90 degrees clockwise	
House	122	A: 1st shape > 3rd shape; 2nd shape > 4th shape &flips; 3rd shape > 2nd shape; 4th shape > 1st shape &flips	

Figure Analogy Questions Answered Correctly: _____ out of 12

COGAT® QUESTION TYPE 8: FIGURE CLASSIFICATION (NON-VERBAL SECTION)

Directions for all Figure Classification questions: The pictures on the top row are alike in a certain way. Look at the pictures on the bottom row. Which picture that is in the bottom row would go best with the pictures that are in the top row?

"Find the row with a(n) ___.	Question	Answer	Child's Answer
(p. 82) *"Find the page where there is a turtle at the bottom."*			
Duck	123	C: shapes that are not rounded	
Bug	124	A: 4 shapes	
Crab	125	D: same shape group rotated (note star position)	
Web	126	D: only 2 dark blue stars are next to each other	
(p. 83) *"Find the page where there is a happy face at the bottom."*			
Fork	127	B: at least 3 stars beside each other (like tic-tac-toe)	
Spoon	128	C: same shape is rotated	
Cup	129	A: outer & inner shapes are different	
Fish	130	D: 6-sided shapes	
(p. 84) *"Find the page where there is a plane at the bottom."*			
Boat	131	A: 1 dark square, 2 white, 1 white w/ light blue shape	
Key	132	C: same shapes opposite each other (2 kinds of shapes)	
Hat	133	D: 3 shapes inside square	
Bug	134	C: 2 of the same shape next to each other	
(p. 85) *"Find the page where there is a cow at the bottom."*			
Key	135	B: diagonal lines going lower left to upper right	
Happy Face	136	A: 3 upside-down triangles,1 right-side up triangle	
Leaf	137	D: small rectangle beside oval inside large diamond	
Heart	138	C: curvy line at same position on "M"/"W" figure (near where straight lines join)	

Figure Classification Questions Answered Correctly: _____ out of 16

COGAT® QUESTION TYPE 9: PAPER FOLDING (NON-VERBAL SECTION)

Directions for all Paper Folding questions: The top row of pictures shows a sheet of paper, how it was folded, and how something was cut out. Look at the bottom row. Which picture shows how the paper would look after it is unfolded?

"Find the row with a(n) __."	Question Number	Answer	Child's Answer
(p. 86) *"Find the page with a horse at the bottom."*			
Car	139	C	
Chair	140	C	
Pencil	141	D	
(p. 87) *"Find the page with a tree at the bottom."*			
Fish	142	A	
Shirt	143	B	
House	144	C	

"Find the row with a(n) __."	Question Number	Answer	Child's Answer
(p. 88) *"Find the page with a stoplight at the bottom."*			
Heart	145	D	
Arrow	146	B	
Crab	147	C	
(p. 89) *"Find the page with a boat at the bottom."*			
Web	148	D	
Truck	149	C	
Boot	150	A	

"Find the row with a(n) __."	Question Number	Answer	Child's Answer
(p. 90) *"Find the page with a heart at the bottom."*			
Triangle	151	D	
Key	152	A	
Leaf	153	C	

Paper Folding Questions Answered Correctly: _____ out of 15

Did your child finish the exercises? Here's a certificate for your child! (Please cut along the dotted lines.)

Great Work!

Congratulations to:

_____